Books written by Jack Hartman

Trust God for Your Finances 1983 (over 175,000 copies in print)
Nuggets of Faith 1984
One Hundred Years from Today 1985
How to Study the Bible 1985
Never, Never Give Up 1994
Quiet Confidence in the Lord 1996

Books co-authored with Judy Hartman

Increased Energy and Vitality 1994
God's Wisdom Is Available to You 2001
Exchange Your Worries for God's Perfect Peace 2003
Unshakable Faith in Almighty God 2004
Receive Healing from the Lord 2006
What Does God Say? 2008
Victory Over Adversity 2009
God's Joy Regardless of Circumstances 2009
A Close and Intimate Relationship with God 2010
Overcoming Fear 2011
Effective Prayer 2011
God's Instructions for Growing Older 2012
You Can Hear the Voice of God 2012
God's Plan for Your Life 2013
Reverent Awe of God 2013
Glorious Eternal Life in Heaven 2014
Live Continually in the Presence of God 2014
The Rapture and the Second Coming of Christ 2015

Scripture Meditation Cards
with accompanying CDs (1996-2000)
co-authored by Jack and Judy Hartman

A Closer Relationship with the Lord
Continually Increasing Faith in God
Enjoy God's Wonderful Peace
Financial Instructions from God
Find God's Will for Your Life
Freedom from Worry and Fear
God Is Always with You
Our Father's Wonderful Love
Receive God's Blessings in Adversity
Receive Healing from the Lord

The Rapture and the Second Coming of Christ

Jack and Judy Hartman

Lamplight Ministries, Inc.,

Dunedin, Florida

Dear readers, we welcome you to *The Rapture and the Second Coming of Christ*. God's love letter to you, the Bible, will come alive to you if you have acknowledged Jesus Christ as your Savior. If you have not yet entered the kingdom of heaven by choosing the gift of eternal salvation that Jesus Christ provided for you on the cross, we invite you to go immediately to Chapter 10 of this book.

You are a body, a mind and a spirit. If you read this book with only your mind, you will not fully understand the scriptural contents of this book. We have written this book in such a way that we believe that the Spirit of God will equip you to understand the events in the Bible that we explain in this book.

We want to keep in touch with you. Please come to our website at www.lamplight.net. We have a link for you to send us a message letting us know if this book has made a difference in your life. We will be blessed to hear from you. We will respond to you. Send us an email at lamplightmin@yahoo.com or write to us at Lamplight Ministries, Inc., P.O. Box 1307, Dunedin, FL, 34697.

We would be pleased to send you our monthly newsletter by mail or email. You can request this newsletter online, by calling 1-800-540-1597 or by writing to us. Our newsletters will keep you updated on whatever book we are writing at that time. Each newsletter contains a message from each of us. We invite you to pray for our outreaches into prisons and jails, to the homeless and to Third World countries.

In addition to the books that we have written, we spent five years writing ten sets of Scripture Meditation Cards. We provide a daily devotional on our website from one of these cards each day. You can request to receive it by email. You also can download the first chapter of each book. All of our foreign translations are available online to download free of charge. Our desire is for you to live each day, experiencing Christ in you, the Hope of glory (see Colossians 1:27).

Copyright 2015

Jack and Judy Hartman

Jack and Judy Hartman

Lamplight Ministries Inc.

PO Box 1307

Dunedin, Florida 34697-2921

Telephone: 1-800-540-1597

FAX: 1-727-784-2980

Website: lamplight.net

Email: lamplightmin@yahoo.com

Facebook: facebook.com/jackandjudylamplight

Twitter: twitter.com/lamplightmin

Blog: lamplightmin.wordpress.com

Ebooks: Go to smashwords.com. Type in "Jack Hartman"

ISBN: 978-0-915445-59-2

Library of Congress Control Number: 2015904857

Dedication

We dedicate this book to Pastor Ebenezer Moses in India. God brought Eb into our lives by a divine appointment. Judy has been to visit him, his family and his ministry, India Gospel Fellowship, seven times. Judy considers him to be the most anointed evangelist she has ever met. He is the founder and president of an organization of pastors in India. He developed a three-year Bible School to train young men and women in India to know God, to know the Bible and to know the practical aspects of ministry.

Pastor Ebenezer translated *Trust God for Your Finances* into the Tamil language. He distributed this translation to almost 2,000 pastors in India. Pastor Ebenezer now is planning to translate *The Rapture and the Second Coming of Christ* into Tamil to teach many Indian pastors at their annual pastors' conference. Please pray for Pastor Ebenezer Moses, his family and for India Gospel Fellowship (www.igfglobal.org).

Eb, we love you and thank our heavenly Father for bringing us together. You are a deep joy in our lives. We love you as a son. We are blessed to be your "Mummy" and "Dad Jack."

Table of Contents

Introduction

We believe that the two most important events that have taken place in the history of mankind are the first coming of Jesus Christ and His ascension into heaven after victoriously rising from the dead. We believe that the two most important events in the future will be the Rapture of the Church and the Second Coming of Christ.

Your life will be changed *immensely* if you are part of the generation that is living on earth when the Rapture of the Church and the subsequent Second Coming of Christ occur. We will explain how, if Jesus Christ is your Savior, you will be caught up into the clouds to meet Him during the Rapture of the Church. From there you will go to heaven for approximately seven years. All Christians then will return to earth with Jesus Christ during His second coming which will occur after approximately seven years of horrible tribulation on earth when God pours out His wrath on unbelievers who have rejected the sacrifice made by Jesus Christ.

The events that we will describe in this book will be life-changing beyond anything that you have experienced in your life to date. "...the natural, nonspiritual man does not accept or welcome or admit into his heart the gifts and teachings and revelations of the Spirit of God, for they are folly (meaningless nonsense) to him; and he is incapable of knowing them [of progressively recognizing, understanding, and becoming better acquainted with them] because they are spiritually discerned and estimated and appreciated. But the spiritual man tries all things [he examines, investigates, inquires into, questions, and discerns all things]..." (I Corinthians 2:14-15)

Most unbelievers will have closed minds on this subject. We are told that unbelievers will not "accept or welcome or admit" these great spiritual truths. The first amplification in this passage of Scripture says that many unbelievers look at the teaching of the Bible as "meaningless nonsense."

A person cannot make a bigger mistake than to disregard the tremendous scriptural truths that we will discuss in this book. The entire world will be changed beyond comprehension by the Rapture of the Church and the Second Coming of Christ. Unbelievers are "incapable" of understanding these great scriptural truths. Only people who have received Jesus Christ as Savior are able to understand the great truths of the Bible.

Before I was saved 40 years ago, I (Jack) attempted to study the Bible. I could not understand what I was trying to study. However, when I received Jesus Christ as my Savior, I suddenly was able to understand Scripture. I could not get enough of God's Word. I studied the holy Scriptures daily and I meditated day and night on the Word of God.

The final amplification in I Corinthians 2:15 instructs us to "examine, investigate and inquire into" scriptural truths. We urge you to make the quality decision to carefully study and meditate on these vitally important scriptural truths pertaining to the Rapture of the Church and the Second Coming of Christ.

We now use *The Amplified Bible* exclusively in our books. I (Jack) have been using *The Amplified Bible* since 1975. At that time only *The Amplified New Testament* was available. I bought this version of the Bible when I saw it in a Christian bookstore because of an inscription from Dr. Billy Graham on the cover. Dr. Graham said, "This is the best Study Testament on the market. It is a magnificent translation. I use it constantly."

The Amplified Bible is the result of the study of a group of Bible scholars who spent a total of more than 20,000 hours amplifying the Bible. They believe that traditional word-by-word translation often fails to reveal the shades of meaning that are part of the original Greek, Hebrew and Aramaic biblical texts.

Their amplification of the original text uses brackets for words that clarify the meaning and parentheses for words that contain additional phrases included in the original language. Through this amplification the reader will gain a better understanding of what Hebrew and Greek listeners instinctively understood.

We would like to give you a specific example of why we use *The Amplified Bible* exclusively:
- "I can do all things through Christ which strengtheneth me." (Philippians 4:13, *The King James Version*)
- "I can do all this through him who gives me strength." (Philippians 4:13, *The New International Version*)

- "I have strength for all things in Christ Who empowers me [I am ready for anything and equal to anything through Him Who infuses inner strength into me; I am self-sufficient in Christ's sufficiency]." (Philippians 4:13, *The Amplified Bible*)

Please note the significant amplification of the original Greek in *The Amplified Bible*. If you make the decision to meditate on Philippians 4:13, you will find that there is much more depth of meaning in *The Amplified Bible* version of this verse.

We recommend that you first read through this book completely. See for yourself exactly what God says about the Rapture of the Church and the Second Coming of Christ.

Then read through the book a second time and highlight or underline all Scripture references and our explanation of this Scripture that is especially meaningful to you. Write notes in the margin or at the top or bottom of each page. If you do, you then will be able to *meditate* on the meaningful passages of Scripture that you have identified as being important to you (see Joshua 1:8 and Psalm 1:2-3).

I (Jack) want to explain why I use the first person on some occasions in our books. I write the first two drafts of each book. Judy then adds her valuable input to the next two drafts. I then write the final two drafts.

I do not want to use the words "I (Jack)" every time I use a first-person reference. I will just use the word "I" whenever I make a personal observation during the remainder of this book. Any personal observations from Judy will be clearly identified.

We blend together our explanations of Scripture. We thank God for the high privilege of dividing His Word, each of us bringing different expertise to create a final book for you. Imagine a husband and wife, each with a bedroom/office at home, working together every day with different viewpoints that God brings together harmoniously. We are blessed beyond words that God has used us in this way since 1991.

We explain each passage of Scripture in simple and easy-to-understand language. We pray that the scriptural contents of this book and our explanation of this Scripture will help you to learn vitally important scriptural truths pertaining to the Rapture of the Church and the Second Coming of Christ.

Chapter 1

God Is the Author of the Bible

In this book we will make some statements that are very extreme. If you are part of the generation that will be living when Jesus Christ returns for His Church, your life will change immediately to a degree that is beyond the limitations of the comprehension of any human being. The world has never seen anything that is remotely like the events that will occur during the Rapture of the Church and the Second Coming of Christ. We pray that you will make the decision to approach what we teach in this book with a completely open mind, no matter how radical some of these statements might seem.

We urge you to study for yourself exactly what the Bible has to say about these two significant events. If you are alive when these events take place, these events will be the most important things that have ever happened to you. Nothing else that you have ever experienced *can even come close* to the magnitude of what will happen in the lives of each person who is alive when Jesus Christ comes for His Church and subsequently comes back to earth for a second time.

I have read more than 30 books pertaining to this topic. These books all have one thing in common – they are *very* complicated and difficult to understand. We do not want to write a book that is filled with minutiae pertaining to the Rapture of the Church and the Second Coming of Christ. We do not want to confuse readers with excessive detail. If you like what you read in this book, you can search the internet for additional books on the Rapture of the Church and the Second Coming of Christ.

A great deal of confusion exists pertaining to these events. We have done our best to explain in simple and easy-to-understand language what the Bible teaches about the Rapture of the Church and the Second Coming of Christ. Most principles that we explain will be solidly anchored on Scripture. Occasionally we will give our opinion. We will clearly state when we are giving our opinion.

Our goal is to write this book in such a manner that a fourth grade student who is a Christian can understand everything in this book. Many Christians do not have a thorough understanding of what the Bible says will take place during the Rapture of the Church and the Second Coming of Christ. In this book we will explain the following events sequentially:

- The Rapture of the Church
- The Judgment Seat of Christ
- The Tribulation
- The Second Coming of Christ
- The Millennium
- The Great White Throne Judgment

Some people believe that there will be no Rapture. We believe that I Thessalonians 4:17 specifically says that there will be a Rapture. Some people believe that Rapture will occur in the middle of the Tribulation. Some people believe that the Rapture will occur at the end of the Tribulation. We believe that the Rapture will occur before the Tribulation. We are writing this book to explain why and where in Scripture we see God's description of the Rapture.

We know that Jesus Christ will come to rapture the Church. We know that He will come to earth again. The only question is *when* these very significant events will take place, not *if* they will take place. Jesus said, "...I will come back again and will take you to Myself, that where I am you may be also." (John 14:3)

In this statement Jesus clearly states that He *will* come back again and that He will take the Church to Himself. The writing of every human author of the Bible was inspired by God. "Every Scripture is God-breathed (given by His inspiration) and profitable for instruction, for reproof and conviction of sin, for correction of error and discipline in obedience, [and] for training in righteousness (in holy living, in conformity to God's will in thought, purpose, and action)" (II Timothy 3:16)

Please note the word "every" at the beginning of this verse. Every word in the Bible comes from God. *God is the Author of the Bible.* In his letter to the Galatians, the apostle Paul said, "...I want you to know, brethren, that the Gospel which was proclaimed and made known by me is not man's gospel [a human invention, according to or patterned after any human standard]. For indeed I did not receive it from man, nor was I taught it, but [it came to me] through a [direct] revelation [given] by Jesus Christ (the Messiah)." (Galatians 1:11-12)

Paul said that every word that he wrote came through a "direct revelation" from Jesus Christ. In his first letter to the Christians in Thessalonica Paul said, "...we also [especially] thank God continually for this, that when you received the message of God [which you heard] from us, you welcomed it not as the word of [mere] men, but as it truly is, the Word of God, which is effectually at work in you who believe [exercising its superhuman power in those who adhere to and trust in and rely on it]." (I Thessalonians 2:13)

The Bible is *not* "the word of mere men." The Bible is the Word of God. The amplification at the end of this verse speaks of the "superhuman power" of the Bible. The supernatural power of God will be released in your life to the degree that you "adhere to and trust in and rely on" the holy Scriptures.

If Jesus Christ is your Savior, you will be able to understand the Bible. "...as many as are the promises of God, they all find their Yes [answer] in Him [Christ]...." (II Corinthians 1:20)

In this chapter we have given you a brief summary of what you will read in the remainder of the book. We now are ready to study exactly what the Bible says about the Rapture of the Church. The next two chapters will explain the immense impact that this event will have on the life of every person who is alive at that time.

Chapter 2

The Rapture of the Church

We will present many astonishing truths from the Bible throughout the remainder of this book. These truths will be totally life-changing for every person who is alive at the time of the Rapture. In Chapter 1 we showed you that, even though we will make some astonishing statements, you can be absolutely certain that these statements are reliable because God is the Author of the Bible. Everything in the Bible is true.

In this chapter we will examine the Rapture of the Church in detail. The word "rapture" is not listed anywhere in the Bible. This word comes from the Latin word "rapio" which means "to snatch away suddenly." The Rapture of the Church will take place when Jesus Christ appears and draws all Christians into the clouds to meet Him. As astonishing as this may seem, you will see that the Bible clearly teaches that this event will occur.

Christian scholars are divided in their opinion as to when the scriptural events that are described in this book will occur. We are presenting the truth as we see it according to the Bible, but we do want you to know that there is some difference of opinion as to when these scriptural events that we describe in this book will occur.

The Rapture is *only* for people who have received eternal salvation through Jesus Christ. Unbelievers will not participate in the Rapture. Jesus said, "...whoever is ashamed [here and now] of Me and My words in this adulterous (unfaithful) and [preeminently] sinful generation, of him will the Son of Man also be ashamed when He comes in the glory (splendor and majesty) of His Father with the holy angels." (Mark 8:38)

We believe that the words "this adulterous, unfaithful and preeminently sinful generation" in this verse and the amplification definitely could apply to our generation. The following *long* passage of Scripture describes exactly what will take place when Jesus Christ raptures the Church. "...we would not have you ignorant, brethren, about those who fall asleep [in death], that you may not grieve [for them] as the rest do who have no hope [beyond the grave]. For since we believe that Jesus died and rose again, even so God will also bring with Him through Jesus those who have fallen asleep [in death]. For this we declare to you by the Lord's [own] word, that we who are alive and remain until the coming of the Lord shall in no way precede [into His presence] or have any advantage at all over those who have previously fallen asleep [in Him in death]. For the Lord Himself will descend from heaven with a loud cry of summons, with the shout of an archangel, and with the blast of the trumpet of God. And those who have departed this life in Christ will rise first. Then we, the living ones who remain [on the earth], shall simultaneously be caught up along with [the resurrected dead] in the clouds to meet the Lord in the air; and so always (through the eternity of the eternities) we shall be with the Lord!" (I Thessalonians 4:13-17)

This passage of Scripture does not refer to the Second Coming of Christ. The Rapture occurs *before* the Second Coming of Christ. In the Rapture Jesus Christ meets all Christians *in the air* between heaven and earth. The Second Coming of Christ occurs when Jesus sets His feet on the Mount of Olives as He *returns to earth*.

Jesus will descend from heaven "with the shout of an archangel and with a blast of the trumpet of God." Every person on earth who has received Jesus Christ as his or her Savior will "simultaneously be caught up along with the resurrected dead in the clouds to meet the Lord in the air."

We have stated that this book will be filled with astonishing statements. As you saw in Chapter 1, there is no question that every word in the Bible is true. I Thessalonians 4:13-17 is true. If God says something in the Bible, these words are unequivocally true, no matter how difficult any statement might be for some people to believe based on their current comprehension.

The Bible teaches that there will be one generation of Christians who will *not* die. These Christians will bypass death as they ascend into the air to meet Jesus Christ and then go with Him to heaven. "Take notice! I tell you a mystery (a secret truth, an event decreed by the hidden purpose or counsel of God). We shall not all fall asleep [in death], but we shall all be changed (transformed) in a moment, in the twinkling of an eye, at the [sound of the] last trumpet call. For a trumpet will sound, and the dead [in Christ] will be raised imperishable (free and immune from decay), and we shall be changed (transformed)." (I Corinthians 15:51-52)

Writing under the anointing of the Holy Spirit, the apostle Paul speaks of a mystery which is described as a "a secret truth" in the amplification of this verse. There is one generation of Christians who will not die. These Christians will be transformed at the sound of the last trumpet. They will join the dead in Christ in the air.

Not only will this amazing event take place, but our bodies will be changed instantaneously as we ascend into the air. Verse 52 says that our perishable bodies will put on an imperishable nature. The perishable bodies that we have on earth cannot live in heaven. Not only will Jesus draw all living and deceased Christians to Him in the air, but He will supernaturally transform all of our bodies into imperishable bodies that are free from decay.

The Rapture of the Church is a tremendous miracle by itself, but when we add the undeniable truth that the bodies of all Christians will be made perfect, we are reading an astounding statement. "...we earnestly and patiently await [the coming of] the Lord Jesus Christ (the Messiah) [as] Savior, Who will transform and fashion anew the body of our humiliation to conform to and be like the body of His glory and majesty, by exerting that power which enables Him even to subject everything to Himself." (Philippians 3:20-21)

This passage of Scripture clearly tells us that Jesus Christ will transform our bodies to be like His body.

He will release His supernatural power to cause this amazing event to take place. Every Christian who died before the Rapture will rise first to meet Jesus in the air. "It is sown a natural (physical) body; it is raised a supernatural (a spiritual) body. [As surely as] there is a physical body, there is also a spiritual body." (I Corinthians 15:44)

The spirits of all Christians who die before the rapture go immediately to heaven. We believe that these Christians receive a heavenly body to go with their souls and their spirits. At the Rapture of the Church these Christians will receive a new glorified body to replace the temporary heavenly bodies that they had in heaven.

The statements that we are making may sound impossible, but *nothing* is impossible for God. The following words that Jesus spoke to His disciples many years ago also are His words to you today. Jesus said, "...With men this is impossible, but all things are possible with God." (Matthew 19:26)

Graves all over the world will open to release the bodies of deceased Christians as Jesus descends from heaven. Most Christians will be taken out of their graves, but some will rise from oceans, lakes and rivers where they drowned. Other Christians who were burned to death, blown up in an explosion or whose bodies were destroyed in other ways will rise from the dead.

The Rapture will be a spectacular event. Christians who are raptured will experience an amazing sight on this glorious day as they are lifted into the sky and see tremendous numbers of other Christians who are joyfully ascending with them.

This chapter has been filled with amazing truths from the Bible. Do you believe that every word in the Bible is true, no matter how astounding some statements may seem? In the remainder of this book you will read many additional statements from the Bible that are completely different from anything you have experienced in your life.

You have seen that God is the Author of the Bible. He *always* tells the truth, no matter how astounding some of these statements may seem. The remainder of this book will be filled with additional statements that will be very difficult to believe with the limitations of your human understanding. "...it is impossible for God ever to prove false or deceive us..." (Hebrews 6:18)

Chapter 3

Glorious Life in Heaven
after the Rapture

In the last chapter you read some of the most astonishing truths in the entire Bible. Some of the statements that we made might be very difficult to comprehend, but each statement about the Rapture of the Church is solidly anchored on Scripture.

After Jesus Christ meets all Christians in the clouds, He then will take all of the raptured Christians with Him to heaven. Christians will be rewarded in heaven for the service that they rendered to God during their lives on earth. Jesus said, "...the Son of Man is going to come in the glory (majesty, splendor) of His Father with His angels, and then He will render account and reward every man in accordance with what he has done." (Matthew 16:27)

This verse explains the transition from the Rapture of the Church to being rewarded in heaven for what you have done to serve the Lord. We believe that this time of reward will be one of the first events that will take place after all of the believers who have been raptured are taken to heaven.

All Christians who have been raptured will appear before The Judgment Seat of Christ. "...we must all appear and be revealed as we are before the judgment seat of Christ, so that each one may receive [his pay] according to what he has done in the body, whether good or evil [considering what his purpose and motive have been, and what he has achieved, been busy with, and given himself and his attention to accomplishing]." (II Corinthians 5:10)

The Judgment Seat of Christ will reveal exactly what each Christian did to serve God during his or her life on earth. You will be judged as to how you spent your time. What was your primary motivation? Was your primary motivation to serve Jesus Christ or to pursue personal goals?

In the next chapter we will explain why we believe that raptured Christians will be with Jesus Christ in heaven for approximately seven years. In a subsequent chapter you will learn from the Bible that all Christians who were raptured will return to earth with Jesus Christ during the Second Coming of Christ. We believe that Christians who were rewarded for exemplary service to the Lord during their lives on earth will serve as leaders during the 1,000-year Millennium that we will describe in a subsequent chapter.

Another event that will take place during the approximately seven years that Christians will be in heaven before returning to earth with Jesus Christ at His second coming will be the Marriage of the Lamb. When Jesus raptures the church, the Rapture actually will culminate with a spiritual marriage between Jesus Christ and His saints who joined Him in the Rapture.

The apostle John was given a vision of this glorious occasion. Writing under the anointing of God John said, "Let us rejoice and shout for joy [exulting and triumphant]! Let us celebrate and ascribe to Him glory and honor, for the marriage of the Lamb [at last] has come, and His bride has prepared herself. She has been permitted to dress in fine (radiant) linen, dazzling and white—for the fine linen is (signifies, represents) the righteousness (the upright, just, and godly living, deeds, and conduct, and right standing with God) of the saints (God's holy people). Then [the angel] said to me, Write this down: Blessed (happy, to be envied) are those who are summoned (invited, called) to the marriage supper of the Lamb. And he said to me [further], These are the true words (the genuine and exact declarations) of God." (Revelation 19:7-9)

This passage of Scripture explains how Jesus Christ will come for His bride, the Church, in the Rapture. A great celebration will take place in heaven. Every Christian who has been raptured will be part of a glorious ceremony with Christ that is called the Marriage Supper of the Lamb.

Heaven is a glorious place. All Christians who have been raptured will enjoy the wondrous blessings of heaven. When you arrive in heaven, you will arrive at your real home. "...we are citizens of the state (commonwealth, homeland) which is in heaven..." (Philippians 3:20)

The glory of heaven is so great that our human vocabulary is insufficient to describe it. "...What eye has not seen and ear has not heard and has not entered into the heart of man, [all that] God has prepared (made and keeps ready) for those who love Him [who hold Him in affectionate reverence, promptly obeying Him and gratefully recognizing the benefits He has bestowed]." (I Corinthians 2:9)

Every person in heaven is filled with joy. "God will wipe away every tear from their eyes; and death shall be no more, neither shall there be anguish (sorrow and mourning) nor grief nor pain any more, for the old conditions and the former order of things have passed away." (Revelation 21:4)

No one in heaven dies. No one in heaven is sad. No one in heaven suffers from pain. No one in heaven cries. God promises to wipe away every tear that any Christian might have had because of problems that he or she faced on earth.

Every person who has received Jesus Christ as his or her Savior has a glorious future. Whether you die and go to heaven or you are raptured, you have a magnificent future ahead of you. We cannot even begin to comprehend with the limitations of our human understanding how great heaven is. Meeting Jesus Christ in the air will be only the beginning of a glorious existence where every Christian will be with Jesus forevermore.

Now that you have read the magnificent truths about the Rapture of the Church and living in heaven, your Father wants you to obey His specific instructions while you await the Rapture of the Church if this glorious event occurs during your lifetime. "It has trained us to reject and renounce all ungodliness (irreligion) and worldly (passionate) desires, to live discreet (temperate, self-controlled), upright, devout (spiritually whole) lives in this present world, awaiting and looking for the [fulfillment, the realization of our] blessed hope, even the glorious appearing of our great God and Savior Christ Jesus (the Messiah, the Anointed One)" (Titus 2:12-13)

Look forward to the possibility that *you* could be among the Christians who will go to heaven without dying in the Rapture. We will explain in detail in subsequent chapters why we believe that our generation very well could be the generation that will be raptured. While you are awaiting the Rapture, God instructs you to reject all ungodliness and worldly desires. Live the remainder of your life on earth as a devout Christian who is looking forward to our "blessed hope" which is the glorious appearing of Jesus Christ in the clouds.

In the last two chapters we have studied what the Bible teaches about the Rapture of the Church and what a glorious event this will be followed by subsequent time in heaven. In the next two chapters we will look carefully into the Word of God to see the *horrible* life that every person who has not received Jesus Christ as his or her Savior will be living during the seven-year Tribulation that will begin on the day that Christians are raptured.

The comparison between the glorious life that Christians will experience and the horrible life that unbelievers will suffer is *astounding*. We urge you to carefully study what the Bible says about the Tribulation that all unbelievers who remain on earth will go through after the Rapture of the Church. If you have not received Jesus Christ as your Savior or if you have friends, family and loved ones who are unbelievers, pray about sharing this information with every person who still has time to surrender his or her life to Jesus Christ (see Chapter 10).

Chapter 4

The Tribulation

In the last two chapters we carefully studied one of the greatest events in the history of mankind. The Rapture of the Church will be a glorious event for every member of the family of God. In the next two chapters we will study what will happen to the unbelievers who are left behind on earth after Jesus Christ draws all Christians into the air to be with Him forevermore.

In the next two chapters we will carefully study what will happen in the approximately seven year period between the time that the Church is raptured and Jesus Christ returns to earth for a second time. This period of time is called the Tribulation. This seven-year period will be *the most horrible time in the history of the world*. Unbelievers will pay a price during the Tribulation that is beyond the limitations of human comprehension.

The following words are an Old Testament prophecy pertaining to the Tribulation. "...there shall be a time of trouble, straitness, and distress such as never was since there was a nation till that time. But at that time your people shall be delivered, everyone whose name shall be found written in the Book [of God's plan for His own]. And many of those who sleep in the dust of the earth shall awake: some to everlasting life and some to shame and everlasting contempt and abhorrence." (Daniel 12:1-2)

This passage of Scripture says that there will be a time of trouble that will be worse than anything the world has known. This passage of Scripture says that God's people will be delivered. It also says that deceased believers will be raised during the Rapture of the Church.

The following verse contrasts the glory of the Rapture of the Church and the horror of the Tribulation. Christians are instructed to "...look forward to and await the coming of His Son from heaven, Whom He raised from the dead—Jesus, Who personally rescues and delivers us out of and from the wrath [bringing punishment] which is coming [upon the impenitent] and draws us to Himself [investing us with all the privileges and rewards of the new life in Christ, the Messiah]." (I Thessalonians 1:10)

Now that you have read the explanation of the Rapture of the Church in the last two chapters, you can look forward to Jesus Christ rapturing *you* if He truly is your Savior. We are told that Jesus will deliver us from the wrath that God will pour out on the unbelievers who are left on earth during the Tribulation.

Some people believe that Christians will go through the Tribulation. We disagree. We believe in the absolute inerrancy of the Bible. You have seen that I Thessalonians 1:10 says that born-again believers will not be on earth during the Tribulation.

Why will unbelievers go through the horrors of the Tribulation? The purpose of the Tribulation is to pour out God's wrath on unbelievers all over the world who have rejected eternal salvation through the Lord Jesus Christ. The Tribulation will "...deal out retribution (chastisement and vengeance) upon those who do not know or perceive or become acquainted with God, and [upon those] who ignore and refuse to obey the Gospel of our Lord Jesus Christ." (II Thessalonians 1:8)

People who ignored what they heard about eternal salvation through Jesus Christ will pay a terrible price for ignoring what God says. God loves *every* person in the world so much that He gave up His beloved Son to pay the full price for the sins of every person. "...God so greatly loved and dearly prized the world that He [even] gave up His only begotten (unique) Son, so that whoever believes in (trusts in, clings to, relies on) Him shall not perish (come to destruction, be lost) but have eternal (everlasting) life." (John 3:16)

God made a tremendous sacrifice by giving up His only Son to leave heaven and come to earth to die a horrible death by crucifixion to pay the full price for the sins of all mankind. Jesus Christ also made a tremendous sacrifice. Jesus "...although being essentially one with God and in the form of God [possessing the fullness of the attributes which make God God], did not think this equality with God was a thing to be eagerly grasped or retained, but stripped Himself [of all privileges and rightful dignity], so as to assume the guise of a servant (slave), in that He became like men and was born a human being. And after He had appeared in human form, He abased and humbled Himself [still further] and carried His obedience to the extreme of death, even the death of the cross!" (Philippians 2:6-8)

We are told here that Jesus Christ is one with God and equal to God. Nevertheless, Jesus willingly came to earth as a servant by being born as a human being. Jesus humbled Himself even more by dying an agonizing death from crucifixion to pay the full price for the sins of every human being.

God sent His beloved Son to earth to pay the price for the sins of every person. Jesus Christ took upon Himself the blackness of all of the sins of every person who ever lived. "For our sake He made Christ [virtually] to be sin Who knew no sin, so that in and through Him we might become [endued with, viewed as being in, and examples of] the righteousness of God [what we ought to be, approved and acceptable and in right relationship with Him, by His goodness]." (II Corinthians 5:21)

You are told here that Jesus Who never sinned actually *became sin*. Every person who accepts the glorious sacrifice of eternal salvation through Jesus Christ will be raptured to live forevermore with Him. Every person who ignores or rejects this great sacrifice will pay the full price for this choice during the Tribulation.

People all over the world will face different situations when Jesus Christ comes in the air to rapture the Church. The Rapture will occur simultaneously at different times in different parts of the world because of the difference in time zones. Christians in parts of the world where the Rapture takes place at night will not even know what happened to them. They will be sleeping in their beds and suddenly they will find themselves flying through the air to begin the greatest experience of their lives.

If one spouse is a born-again believer and the other is not, the unbelieving spouse will wake up to find that his or her spouse has disappeared. A husband and wife in one part of the world can be eating lunch when suddenly the wife will disappear. Many families will be divided during the Rapture of the Church. *Chaos will reign* as family members who have been left behind agonize over the sudden disappearance of other members of their families.

Consider what will happen in other places during the Rapture of the Church. Visualize a hospital where surgeons are performing operations. In one operating room the surgeon suddenly will disappear. In another operating room the patient could suddenly disappear. Some of the attending nurses could disappear. The president of the United States could be conducting a cabinet meeting when suddenly the president (if he is a Christian) will disappear. Some members of the cabinet may disappear. Governments all over the world will be in disarray when key leaders disappear.

We believe that many airplanes will crash. Pilots who are Christians will disappear. Many seats on airliners suddenly will be empty as some passengers who are Christians disappear. The world will be in an extreme state of disarray. Chaos will prevail.

Visualize the large number of automobile accidents that very likely will take place all over the earth. Our busy highways will be littered with wreckage as Christian drivers suddenly will disappear. The cars which are out of control will collide with other cars, people and buildings.

Try to visualize what the first day of the Tribulation will be like. Life as we know it will change tremendously. People will be bewildered by the accidents, the crashes, the missing family members and other people who have suddenly disappeared. The chaos that will prevail on earth will be *impossible* for us to comprehend. People who rejected eternal salvation through Jesus Christ will pay an incomprehensible price during the first few days of the Tribulation. This price will get worse during the remainder of the Tribulation.

Jesus prophesied about the severity of the Tribulation when He said, "...then there will be great tribulation (affliction, distress, and oppression) such as has not been from the beginning of the world until now—no, and never will be [again]." (Matthew 24:21)

The world has never experienced anything remotely like the Tribulation. God will pour out His wrath on people who have rejected or ignored the great sacrifice that He and His Son made.

The ordeals that people will go through during the Tribulation will be *so* severe that many people will wish to die. "...in those days people will seek death and will not find it; and they will yearn to die, but death evades and flees from them." (Revelation 9:6)

We do not like having to write this chapter. However, there is no question about the extreme severity of the price that people will pay during the Tribulation. In the next chapter we will study in detail exactly what the Bible says will take place during the Tribulation. We will study what the Bible says about the emergence of the Antichrist and what will happen during the period of time when he deceives people on earth and temporarily becomes their leader.

We pray that many people who are reading these words will receive Jesus Christ as their Savior before it is too late. If you are not absolutely certain that Jesus Christ is your Savior and that you will be caught up into the air to join Him during the Rapture of the Church, we explain in Chapter 10 exactly what the Bible instructs you to do to receive eternal salvation through Jesus Christ. Carefully study what the Bible says about the greatest decision you will ever make. You can live with Jesus Christ throughout eternity instead of having to pay the horrible price that all unbelievers will pay during the Tribulation.

Chapter 5

The Antichrist

The Tribulation will last for seven years. An evil man will rise up during the Tribulation. The Bible refers to him as the Antichrist.

Sometimes the Antichrist is referred to by the name of "the beast." Unbelievers on earth after the Rapture of the Church will have great admiration for the Antichrist. They will trust him to solve the horrible problems that they face. "...the whole earth went after the beast in amazement and admiration." (Revelation 13:3)

The unbelievers who were left behind will worship the Antichrist. They will look at him as if he is God. They "...fell down and paid homage to the dragon, because he had bestowed on the beast all his dominion and authority; they also praised and worshiped the beast, exclaiming, Who is a match for the beast, and, Who can make war against him?" (Revelation 13:4)

Satan will give the Antichrist power during the first half of the Tribulation. "... the beast was given the power of speech, uttering boastful and blasphemous words, and he was given freedom to exert his authority and to exercise his will during forty-two months (three and a half years)." (Revelation 13:5)

The Antichrist will have a tremendous influence on the world during the Tribulation. The prefix "anti" means "against." Everything that the Antichrist will do during the Tribulation will consist of acts that are in opposition to Jesus Christ. "...many imposters (seducers, deceivers, and false leaders) have gone out into the world, men who will not acknowledge (confess, admit) the coming of Jesus Christ (the Messiah) in bodily form. Such a one is the imposter (the seducer, the deceiver, the false leader, the antagonist of Christ) and the Antichrist." (II John 1:7)

The amplification in this verse says that the Antichrist will be a "deceiver and a false leader." He will do everything possible to deceive all of the unbelievers who are left on earth during the Tribulation. The Bible describes the Antichrist as "...the man of lawlessness (sin) is revealed, who is the son of doom (of perdition), who opposes and exalts himself so proudly and insolently against and over all that is called God or that is worshiped, [even to his actually] taking his seat in the temple of God, proclaiming that he himself is God." (II Thessalonians 2:3-4)

The Antichrist is in complete opposition to God. He will say that he is God. "The coming [of the lawless one, the Antichrist] is through the activity and working of Satan and will be attended by power and with all sorts of [pretended] miracles and signs and delusive marvels—[all of them] lying wonders..." (II Thessalonians 2:9)

Satan will try to oppose God for one final time during the Tribulation. The Antichrist will be controlled by Satan. He will seem to perform miracles. The Bible asks a question about the Antichrist. "Who is [such a] liar as he who denies that Jesus is the Christ (the Messiah)? He is the Antichrist (the antagonist of Christ), who [habitually] denies and refuses to acknowledge the Father and the Son." (I John 2:22)

People on earth during the Tribulation will be spiritually immature. They will yearn to find relief from the horrible ordeal they are experiencing. The Antichrist will seem to be their only hope. "...all the inhabitants of the earth will fall down in adoration and pay him homage, everyone whose name has not been recorded in the Book of Life of the Lamb that was slain [in sacrifice] from the foundation of the world." (Revelation 13:8)

No person will be able to buy or sell any merchandise during the Tribulation unless that person has the mark of the Antichrist which is "666" on his or her right hand or forehead. "Also he compels all [alike], both small and great, both the rich and the poor, both free and slave, to be marked with an inscription [stamped] on their right hands or on their foreheads, so that no one will have power to buy or sell unless he bears the stamp (mark, inscription), [that is] the name of the beast or the number of his name. Here is [room for] discernment [a call for the wisdom of interpretation]. Let anyone who has intelligence (penetration and insight enough) calculate the number of the beast, for it is a human number [the number of a certain man]; his number is 666." (Revelation 13:16-18)

In the last two chapters we have studied many verses of Scripture that explain what will take place during the Tribulation. In the next chapter we will study Scripture references pertaining to the Second Coming of Christ.

Chapter 6

The Return of Jesus Christ

Some people do not understand the difference between the Rapture of the Church and the Second Coming of Christ. Jesus Christ will not return to earth during the Rapture. He meets all Christians *in the clouds* (see I Thessalonians 4:17). In the Second Coming, Jesus returns to *earth*. In the Rapture Jesus comes *for* His saints. In the Second Coming He comes *with* His saints.

Jesus Christ will return to earth at the same place where He left the world to ascend into heaven at the end of His earthly ministry. The disciples watched Jesus ascend into heaven. "...even as they were looking [at Him], He was caught up, and a cloud received and carried Him away out of their sight. And while they were gazing intently into heaven as He went, behold, two men [dressed] in white robes suddenly stood beside them, who said, Men of Galilee, why do you stand gazing into heaven? This same Jesus, Who was caught away and lifted up from among you into heaven, will return in [just] the same way in which you saw Him go into heaven. Then [the disciples] went back to Jerusalem from the hill called Olivet, which is near Jerusalem, [only] a Sabbath day's journey (three-quarters of a mile) away." (Acts 1:9-12)

This passage of Scripture describes the ascension of Jesus Christ from the Mount of Olives to heaven. Jesus will return to earth at the Mount of Olives. "...His feet shall stand in that day upon the Mount of Olives, which lies before Jerusalem on the east, and the Mount of Olives shall be split in two from the east to the west by a very great valley; and half of the mountain shall remove toward the north and half of it toward the south." (Zechariah 14:4)

The Mount of Olives is located to the east of Jerusalem. The return of Christ will be *so* powerful that the Mount of Olives will be split in two. One-half of the former mountain will be moved to the north. The other half will be moved to the south. The supernatural power of Christ's return will cause an enormous valley to be formed between the two portions of the mountain.

We now will look again at a verse of Scripture that we studied in Chapter 3. The Bible refers to the return of Christ as "...the glorious appearing of our great God and Savior Christ Jesus (the Messiah, the Anointed One)." (Titus 2:13)

The return of Jesus Christ will be spectacular. Jesus knew what His return would be like while He was still on earth. He said, "...like the lightning, that flashes and lights up the sky from one end to the other, so will the Son of Man be in His [own] day." (Luke 17:24)

Please note the words "lights up the sky from one end to the other" in this verse. The Second Coming of Christ will be vastly different from the first time He came to earth. When Jesus came the first time, He was born as a human being in a stable surrounded by animals. When He comes the second time, His glorious return will light up the sky. "Immediately after the tribulation of those days the sun will be darkened, and the moon will not shed its light, and the stars will fall from the sky, and the powers of the heavens will be shaken. Then the sign of the Son of Man will appear in the sky, and then all the tribes of the earth will mourn and beat their breasts and lament in anguish, and they will see the Son of Man coming on the clouds of heaven with power and great glory [in brilliancy and splendor]." (Matthew 24:29-30)

Everything will become dark when the Tribulation draws to a close. Suddenly, in the midst of this darkness, Jesus Christ will return to earth in a blaze of light. His return will be signified by the words inscribed on the robe that He will wear when He returns. These words will signify that Jesus Christ is much greater than any person who has ever been a king on earth and much greater than any person who has had the title of lord. "...on His garment (robe) and on His thigh He has a name (title) inscribed, King of kings and Lord of lords." (Revelation 19:16)

When Jesus returns in glory, *you* will be with Him if He is your Savior. You will return with Him in the air just as you ascended to Him in the air during the Rapture of the Church. If Jesus Christ is your Savior, you can look forward to two glorious trips with Him in the air from earth to heaven and from heaven back to earth. You will have lived for seven glorious years in heaven with Jesus before you return to earth with Him.

"...Behold, the Lord comes with His myriads of holy ones (ten thousands of His saints)..." (Jude 1:14)

You have so much to look forward to if Jesus Christ is your Savior. While the earth is going through the anguish of the Tribulation, all Christians will be in heaven with Jesus and then return to earth with Him. Try to visualize the glorious return of an enormous number of Christians to earth at the end of the seven-year Tribulation.

In addition to the Christians who were in heaven with Jesus during the seven years of the Tribulation, other Christians will be waiting for Jesus when He returns. Many people who will go through the horror of the Tribulation will receive Jesus Christ as their Savior during the Tribulation. They will realize the mistake that they made by not making this decision before going through this terrible ordeal. "...one of the elders [of the heavenly Sanhedrin] said, Who are these [people] clothed in the long white robes? And from where have they come? I replied, Sir, you know. And he said to me, These are they who have come out of the great tribulation (persecution), and have washed their robes and made them white in the blood of the Lamb." (Revelation 7:13-14)

People who receive Jesus Christ as Savior during the Tribulation will be wearing long white robes when He returns to earth. These robes will signify that they were cleansed by the blood of Jesus Christ during the Tribulation. These new Christians will join Jesus and the Christians who return with Him.

The Tribulation will end with the Battle of Armageddon. This battle will begin and end in one day.

When Jesus returns to earth, this battle will be fought between Jesus and his followers and the Antichrist and his followers. The apostle John was given a vision of this battle. He said, "Then I saw the beast and the rulers and leaders of the earth with their troops mustered to go into battle and make war against Him Who is mounted on the horse and against His troops. And the beast was seized and overpowered, and with him the false prophet who in his presence had worked wonders and performed miracles by which he led astray those who had accepted or permitted to be placed upon them the stamp (mark) of the beast and those who paid homage and gave divine honors to his statue. Both of them were hurled alive into the fiery lake that burns and blazes with brimstone." (Revelation 19:19-20)

This battle will end quickly because it is a battle between the Antichrist who is a deceiver with no spiritual power and Jesus Christ Who has all spiritual power. Jesus said, "...All authority (all power of rule) in heaven and on earth has been given to Me." (Matthew 28:18)

If a battle is fought between someone who has all power and someone who has no power, this is a battle in name only. That is what the Battle of Armageddon will be.

At the end of the Battle of Armageddon, the Antichrist and the false prophet will be hurled alive into the lake of fire where they will suffer throughout eternity for their evil deeds. When Jesus returns, the unbelievers who are on earth at the end of the Tribulation will pay a significant price for not receiving eternal salvation through Him. "...when the Lord Jesus is revealed from heaven with His mighty angels in a flame of fire, to deal out retribution (chastisement and vengeance) upon those who do not know or perceive or become acquainted with God, and [upon those] who ignore and refuse to obey the Gospel of our Lord Jesus Christ. Such people will pay the penalty and suffer the punishment of everlasting ruin (destruction and perdition) and eternal exclusion and banishment from the presence of the Lord and from the glory of His power" (II Thessalonians 1:7-9)

Jesus will return in a flame of fire. People on earth who still have not received Him as Savior will suffer immensely as they are banished from the presence of the Lord throughout eternity.

The seven-year Tribulation will come to a close. The Millennium will begin at this time. A glorious 1,000-year period of peace will begin. In the next chapter we will study what the Bible teaches about what the earth will be like during the Millennium.

Chapter 7

The Millennium

The Millennium will begin immediately after Jesus Christ comes to earth for the second time. The word "millennium" comes from two Latin words "mille" which means one thousand and "annum" which means year.

The words "one thousand years" are mentioned six times in the 20th chapter of Revelation. Jesus Christ will return to earth in power and glory to establish His kingdom on earth for 1,000 years. This 1,000-year period will be exactly the opposite of the Tribulation. The Millennium will be a time of great peace and joy on earth.

Everything on earth will be so peaceful during the Millennium that all animals will live peacefully together. The prophet Isaiah said, "...the wolf shall dwell with the lamb, and the leopard shall lie down with the kid, and the calf and the young lion and the fatted domestic animal together; and a little child shall lead them. And the cow and the bear shall feed side by side, their young shall lie down together, and the lion shall eat straw like the ox. And the sucking child shall play over the hole of the asp, and the weaned child shall put his hand on the adder's den. They shall not hurt or destroy in all My holy mountain, for the earth shall be full of the knowledge of the Lord as the waters cover the sea." (Isaiah 11:6)

Wild animals no longer will be predators. Wolves will be as gentle as lambs. Lions will lie side-by-side with domestic animals. Little children will not need to be afraid of what any animal might do to them.

There will be not any wars during the Millennium. Peace will reign on earth throughout this period of time. "...nation shall not lift up sword against nation, neither shall they learn war any more." (Micah 4:3)

Please stop and think about how long 1,000 years is. If you can visualize a person living to the age of 90 years, 1,000 years will cover the entire lifespan of 11 people who live to the age of 90. One thousand years is a long time.

If Jesus Christ is your Savior, you will come back with Him when He returns to earth. You will enjoy this glorious 1,000-year period. Satan will not be present during the Millennium.

When the apostle John was caught up into heaven, he was given a vision of what would happen to Satan during the Millennium. John said, "Then I saw an angel descending from heaven; he was holding the key of the Abyss (the bottomless pit) and a great chain was in his hand. And he gripped and overpowered the dragon, that old serpent [of primeval times], who is the devil and Satan, and [securely] bound him for a thousand years. Then he hurled him into the Abyss (the bottomless pit) and closed it and sealed it above him, so that he should no longer lead astray and deceive and seduce the nations until the thousand years were at an end. After that he must be liberated for a short time." (Revelation 20:1-3)

An angel of God will overcome Satan and hurl him into a bottomless pit for the 1,000-year period of the Millennium. Satan will not be able to cause the problems that he was able to create during the final years before the Rapture of the Church.

Jesus Christ will be in complete control throughout the Millennium. The apostle John went on to explain the vision that he was given in regard to what would take place after Satan was thrown into the bottomless pit. John said, "Then I saw thrones, and sitting on them were those to whom authority to act as judges and to pass sentence was entrusted. Also I saw the souls of those who had been slain with axes [beheaded] for their witnessing to Jesus and [for preaching and testifying] for the Word of God, and who had refused to pay homage to the beast or his statue and had not accepted his mark or permitted it to be stamped on their foreheads or on their hands. And they lived again and ruled with Christ (the Messiah) a thousand years." (Revelation 20:4)

Christians who return to earth with Jesus Christ will rule and reign with Him throughout the Millennium. People who came to Christ during the Tribulation and refused to accept the 666 mark of the Antichrist also will rule and reign with Christ.

Old Testament saints who died long ago will be supernaturally located and restored to life. From that moment on, none of these believers will ever be separated from Jesus Christ again. Old Testament saints and New Testament believers will live in harmony throughout eternity. "The remainder of the dead were not restored to life again until the thousand years were completed. This is the first resurrection. Blessed (happy, to be envied) and holy (spiritually whole, of unimpaired innocence and proved virtue) is the person who takes part (shares) in the first resurrection! Over them the second death exerts no power or authority, but they shall be ministers of God and of Christ (the Messiah), and they shall rule along with Him a thousand years." (Revelation 20:5-6)

Satan will make one final effort at the end of the Millennium to do battle with Jesus Christ and His followers. "And when the thousand years are completed, Satan will be released from his place of confinement, and he will go forth to deceive and seduce and lead astray the nations which are in the four quarters of the earth—Gog and Magog—to muster them for war; their number is like the sand of the sea. And they swarmed up over the broad plain of the earth and encircled the fortress (camp) of God's people (the saints) and the beloved city; but fire descended from heaven and consumed them. Then the devil who had led them astray [deceiving and seducing them] was hurled into the fiery lake of burning brimstone, where the beast and false prophet were; and they will be tormented day and night forever and ever (through the ages of the ages)." (Revelation 20:7-10)

The words "Gog and Magog" in this passage of Scripture refer to people who will oppose God. Satan and his followers will lose again to Jesus Christ. After their defeat, Satan and his followers will be hurled into the lake of fire to join the Antichrist and the false prophet. They will suffer horribly throughout eternity in this terrible place that burns with the stifling odor of sulphur.

The Great White Throne Judgment will take place at the end of the Millennium. All unbelievers will be judged at this time. The apostle John was given a vision of this judgment. John said, "Then I saw a great white throne and the One Who was seated upon it, from Whose presence and from the sight of Whose face earth and sky fled away, and no place was found for them. I [also] saw the dead, great and small; they stood before the throne, and books were opened. Then another book was opened, which is [the Book] of Life. And the dead were judged (sentenced) by what they had done [their whole way of feeling and acting, their aims and endeavors] in accordance with what was recorded in the books. And the sea delivered up the dead who were in it, death and Hades (the state of death or disembodied existence) surrendered the dead in them, and all were tried and their cases determined by what they had done [according to their motives, aims, and works]. Then death and Hades (the state of death or disembodied existence) were thrown into the lake of fire. This is the second death, the lake of fire. And if anyone's [name] was not found recorded in the Book of Life, he was hurled into the lake of fire." (Revelation 20:11-15)

Unbelievers will be raised from the dead at this time. After the Great White Throne Judgment, they will join Satan and his demons and the Antichrist and the false prophet in the lake of fire throughout eternity. The word "great" in this passage of Scripture is used because of the majesty of God Who will judge unrepentance at that time. The word "white" represents the holiness and purity of God. Every person whose name is not listed in the Lamb's Book of Life will be judged and then hurled into the lake of fire to be separated throughout eternity from God, Jesus Christ and all Christians.

The purpose of this book has been to explain the Rapture of the Church and the Second Coming of Christ. We believe that we have done this in simple and easy-to-understand language. The Second Coming of Christ will be complete at the end of the Millennium.

The remainder of this book will be dedicated to studying what the Bible teaches about *when* the Rapture of the Church and the Second Coming of Christ will take place. We believe that these great events definitely can take place during the lives of people who are alive in this generation.

Chapter 8

When Will These Events Take Place?

If Jesus Christ is your Savior, we believe that there is a good chance that you will never die. The Bible gives us specific details explaining what life will be like during the last days before the Rapture and the Second Coming of Christ.

Some people mock the return of Jesus Christ. "...you must know and understand this, that scoffers (mockers) will come in the last days with scoffing, [people who] walk after their own fleshly desires and say, Where is the promise of His coming? For since the forefathers fell asleep, all things have continued exactly as they did from the beginning of creation." (II Peter 3:3-4)

Please note that the Bible prophesied almost 2,000 years ago that, in the last days before the Rapture and the Second Coming of Christ, some people will scoff at the return of Jesus Christ. The word "scoff" means to mock, taunt or deride. People who scoff at the return of Jesus Christ are concerned primarily with worldly goals and desires, not the return of Christ.

When these words were written almost 2,000 years ago the apostle Peter, writing under the anointing of the Holy Spirit, knew that Jesus Christ would not return for a long time. He prophesied that people would show contempt for the return of Christ because so many years would go by without His return.

God's ways are very different and very much higher than the ways of the world (see Isaiah 55:8-9). God's timing is very different from the timing of human beings. Shortly after the statement that we have just read Peter wrote, "...do not let this one fact escape you, beloved, that with the Lord one day is as a thousand years and a thousand years as one day. The Lord does not delay and is not tardy or slow about what He promises, according to some people's conception of slowness, but He is long-suffering (extraordinarily patient) toward you, not desiring that any should perish, but that all should turn to repentance." (II Peter 3:8-9)

Even though a long time has elapsed from a human perspective, from God's eternal perspective just a little over two days have gone by. God knows exactly what He is doing. The amplification in this passage of Scripture says that God is "extraordinarily patient." He wants every possible person to hear the message of eternal salvation through Jesus Christ, to repent of his or her sins and to receive eternal salvation. Jesus said, "...this good news of the kingdom (the Gospel) will be preached throughout the whole world as a testimony to all the nations, and then will come the end." (Matthew 24:14)

Jesus said that the message of eternal salvation must be preached throughout the world before His return. God knows exactly how many people have heard of eternal salvation through Jesus Christ. God is omniscient. He is fully aware of every minute detail pertaining to the lives of every person in the world. The psalmist David said, "O Lord, you have searched me [thoroughly] and have known me. You know my downsitting and my uprising; You understand my thought afar off. You sift and search out my path and my lying down, and You are acquainted with all my ways. For there is not a word in my tongue [still unuttered], but, behold, O Lord, You know it altogether." (Psalm 139:1-4)

God knows exactly what every person in the entire world is thinking. He knows when every person goes to bed at night and awakens in the morning. He even knows every word that every person in the world is about to speak before these words are spoken. God knows every minute detail about the life of every person who has ever lived.

God knows every person in the world who has heard the message of eternal salvation through Jesus Christ. God knows exactly how many people have accepted Jesus Christ as Savior and how many people have not received glorious eternal salvation through His Son.

In Chapter 4 we studied John 3:16. This verse explains that God made an enormous sacrifice so that every person would have the opportunity to live with Him throughout eternity. God loves every person in the world *so much* that He gave up His only Son to leave His exalted position in heaven to come to earth as a human being. God loves the world so much that He sent His only Son to die a horrible death by crucifixion to pay the full price for the sins of every person.

Jesus Christ also paid an enormous price so that every person could live throughout eternity with Him. We saw when we studied Philippians 2:5-8 in Chapter 4 that Jesus left His exalted position in heaven to come to earth as a mere human being where He died an agonizing death by crucifixion to pay for the sins of all mankind. The virgin birth of Jesus Christ guaranteed that He was the only person who ever lived who was not a descendant of Adam and Eve.

We saw in Psalm 139:1 at the beginning of this chapter that God is omniscient. God knows whether or not every person on earth has received Jesus Christ as his or her Savior or rejected eternal salvation. We believe that the time is drawing close where God will specifically identify those who have heard of eternal salvation through Jesus Christ and rejected the supreme sacrifice of His beloved Son. We believe that these people will be left behind when the Rapture of the Church occurs.

Jesus Christ instructs all Christians to be ready for His return. He said, "You also must be ready, for the Son of Man is coming at an hour and a moment when you do not anticipate it." (Luke 12:40)

Even though Jesus spoke these words to His disciples many years ago, these words were meant to apply specifically to the generation of people who would be alive when the Rapture of the Church is imminent. Jesus said, "...of that [exact] day and hour no one knows, not even the angels of heaven, nor the Son, but only the Father." (Matthew 24:36)

God has been very patient. The time could be approaching where He finally will pour out His wrath on all of the people who have rejected the supreme sacrifice of His beloved Son. We believe that the time is near when these people will be left behind on earth to go through the horrors of the Tribulation while all people who have received Jesus Christ as their Savior will be raptured and rise into the clouds to meet their beloved Savior.

In the next chapter we will study Scripture that will explain what conditions on earth will be like just before the Rapture of the Church. You can judge for yourself how accurately these specific words portray our generation and how likely it is that Christians in this generation will be raptured to meet Jesus Christ in the clouds. Unbelievers will be left behind to go through the horrors of the Tribulation.

Chapter 9

What Does the Bible Say about the Last Days?

The Rapture of the Church could be imminent. In this chapter we will share several Scripture references and corresponding facts about the world today. This information has led us to conclude that the time for the Rapture of the Church could be drawing near.

God has told His children how He wants us to live while we are preparing for the Rapture. We now will look again at a verse of Scripture that we studied in Chapter 3. "...reject and renounce all ungodliness (irreligion) and worldly (passionate) desires, to live discreet (temperate, self-controlled), upright, devout (spiritually whole) lives in this present world, awaiting and looking for the [fulfillment, the realization of our] blessed hope, even the glorious appearing of our great God and Savior Christ Jesus (the Messiah, the Anointed One)" (Titus 2:12-13)

If there ever was a time when Christians should live godly lives, we live in that time. Our Father instructs us to "reject and renounce all ungodliness" while we await our "blessed hope," the glorious appearance of Jesus Christ in the clouds as He comes for His church.

We believe that God gave us these specific instructions because the world on the whole today is living in a way that is very different from the instructions we have just read. The following long passage of Scripture explains exactly what people will be like in the generation where God raptures His Church and allows all unbelievers to go through the Tribulation. "...understand this, that in the last days will come (set in) perilous times of great stress and trouble [hard to deal with and hard to bear]. For people will be lovers of self and [utterly] self-centered, lovers of money and aroused by an inordinate [greedy] desire for wealth, proud and arrogant and contemptuous boasters. They will be abusive (blasphemous, scoffing), disobedient to parents, ungrateful, unholy and profane. [They will be] without natural [human] affection (callous and inhuman), relentless (admitting of no truce or appeasement); [they will be] slanderers (false accusers, troublemakers), intemperate and loose in morals and conduct, uncontrolled and fierce, haters of good. [They will be] treacherous [betrayers], rash, [and] inflated with self-conceit. [They will be] lovers of sensual pleasures and vain amusements more than and rather than lovers of God." (II Timothy 3:1-4)

Please read these words carefully. Ask yourself if these words that were written almost 2,000 years ago accurately describe what the world is like today.

The world today is very different than it was in previous generations. We are old enough to remember what the world was like when our parents and our grandparents were our age. We believe that selfishness and self-centeredness in the world are *much* more prevalent than just a few years ago. People on the whole today are more greedy and money-oriented than they were in previous generations.

Many people today are "proud, arrogant and contemptuous." The profanity that we hear so often today is much worse than when our parents and grandparents were our age.

We will explain in detail why the words "loose in morals" in this passage of Scripture are more descriptive of the world today than ever before. The last sentence in this passage of Scripture says that many people in the end times generation will love pleasure and amusement more than they love God.

We believe that the tremendous increase in homosexuality in our generation is a definite sign that we live in the last days before the Rapture of the Church and the Tribulation. Homosexuality is perceived as an acceptable lifestyle by many people in our generation. Recent polls indicate that almost 50% of all adults and more than 80% of all high school seniors consider homosexuality to be an acceptable lifestyle. The demand for same-sex marriages has increased tremendously.

How does the significant emphasis on homosexuality in our generation compare with what the Word of God says about homosexuality? The Bible refers to homosexuality as "...vile affections and degrading passions. For their women exchanged their natural function for an unnatural and abnormal one, and the men also turned from natural relations with women and were set ablaze (burning out, consumed) with lust for one another—men committing shameful acts with men and suffering in their own bodies and personalities the inevitable consequences and penalty of their wrong-doing and going astray, which was [their] fitting retribution." (Romans 1:26-27)

Paul in his letter to the saints in Rome almost 2,000 years ago referred to lesbians as being "unnatural and abnormal." The Bible refers to homosexuals as men who "turn from natural relations with women" to be consumed with lust for other men. Romans 1:27 says that homosexuality is a "shameful act." This verse says that homosexuals will pay "the inevitable consequences and penalty of their wrong-doing and going astray."

Even though the Bible says that homosexuality is "vile," "degrading" and "unnatural," 35 of the 50 states in the United States have legalized same-sex marriage at the time this book is written. Gay rights parades have become commonplace in our generation. Many people advocate gay rights.

We believe that another indication that our generation lives in the last days before Jesus Christ returns for His Church is the tremendous increase in abortions in recent years. The majority of these abortions have been caused by selfish sexual desires that result in unwanted pregnancies. At this time more than *40 million abortions* are performed in the world *each year*.

Abortion has been legal in the United States for more than 40 years. In 1973 the United States Supreme Court's Roe v Wade decision legalized abortion in this country.

Advocates of abortion say that abortion is not murder. They say that a fetus is not a human being. What does the Bible say about this? The psalmist said, "...You did form my inward parts; You did knit me together in my mother's womb. I will confess and praise You for You are fearful and wonderful and for the awful wonder of my birth! Wonderful are Your works, and that my inner self knows right well. My frame was not hidden from You when I was being formed in secret [and] intricately and curiously wrought [as if embroidered with various colors] in the depths of the earth [a region of darkness and mystery]. Your eyes saw my unformed substance, and in Your book all the days [of my life] were written before ever they took shape, when as yet there was none of them."(Psalm 139:13-16)

God intricately forms and knits together a baby in the womb of a woman. God obviously does not look at a fetus the way that many people do today. We are told that God has a specific plan for every day of the life of each "unformed substance." Abortion is murder. Legalized abortion violates one of God's Ten Commandments that says, "You shall not commit murder." (Exodus 20:13)

Our federal government has made killing babies legal. How long can we expect God to bless the United States when our federal government legally sanctions the murders of millions of innocent babies?

Our information on abortion in this chapter has referred to the United States. The same trend is taking place throughout the world. On the day that we write these words usabortionclock.org says that

1,357,725,543 abortions have been performed worldwide. More than 38 million abortions have been performed in the world during the year that this book is written.

We believe that another clear sign that our generation is living in the last days before Jesus Christ comes for His church is the significant increase in the number of divorces in our generation. The Bible tells us exactly what God thinks of divorce. "...the Lord, the God of Israel, says: I hate divorce and marital separation" (Malachi 2:16)

God hates divorce because divorce specifically violates what most people say before God when they are married. Most people say that they are being married "for richer or poorer, for better or worse, until death do us part."

Divorce obviously ends a marriage before one of the married partners dies. We want to emphatically state that every person who has been divorced is *not* wrong before God. These people have biblical reasons for divorce. Nevertheless, God hates divorce even though some people who have been divorced are completely innocent before Him.

In this chapter we have compared several Scripture references pertaining to the last days with conditions that exist in the world during our generation. We want to emphasize once again that we believe that our generation could be the generation where God pours out His wrath on unbelievers.

Is God ready to pour out His wrath on this generation? Only God can answer this question. We pray that every person reading this book will be absolutely certain that he or she *will* be raptured with the Church if God makes this decision during our lifetime.

Chapter 10

Will You Live Eternally with Jesus Christ?

We would like to begin this chapter by asking you *the most important question* that anyone will ever ask you. This question is, "Are you *absolutely certain* where you will go when you die, or if you are alive during the Rapture of the Church and the ensuing seven-year Tribulation?

What could possibly be more important than where you will live *throughout eternity*? Will you live eternally in the glory of heaven or suffer eternally in the lake of fire? If the Rapture occurs in your lifetime, will you meet Jesus Christ in the clouds, go to heaven with Him and be with Him forever? Or will you suffer through the seven excruciating years of the Tribulation? If you cannot answer the questions that we have asked, we pray that you will answer these questions affirmatively after you have read this chapter.

We would like to begin this chapter by again studying a very important passage of Scripture that we studied in Chapter 4. The Bible, speaking of Jesus

Christ, says "...[Let Him be your example in humility:] Who, although being essentially one with God and in the form of God [possessing the fullness of the attributes which make God God], did not think this equality with God was a thing to be eagerly grasped or retained, but stripped Himself [of all privileges and rightful dignity], so as to assume the guise of a servant (slave), in that He became like men and was born a human being. And after He had appeared in human form, He abased and humbled Himself [still further] and carried His obedience to the extreme of death, even the death of the cross!" (Philippians 2:5-8)

Jesus Christ turned completely away from His exalted position in heaven to come to earth as a human being. He died a horrible death by crucifixion to pay the full price for *your* sins. "...Christ [the Messiah Himself] died for sins once for all, the Righteous for the unrighteous (the Just for the unjust, the Innocent for the guilty), that He might bring us to God...." (I Peter 3:18)

Jesus Christ, the Messiah, Who never sinned died to pay the full price for your sins so that He could bring you to God. The following words describe the agony that Jesus experienced in His humanity as He anticipated the horrible crucifixion that awaited Him. "...He fell on the ground and kept praying that if it were possible the [fatal] hour might pass from Him. And He was saying, Abba, [which means] Father, everything is possible for You. Take away this cup from Me; yet not what I will, but what You [will]." (Mark 14:35-36)

Jesus asked God if there was any way that He could escape paying the excruciating price that He soon would have to pay when He would be crucified. He then told God that He would do what God desired instead of what He desired in His humanity.

We studied II Corinthians 5:21 in Chapter 4. This verse tells us that Jesus Christ Who never sinned actually *became sin*. Even though Jesus lived a perfect life during His earthly ministry and never once sinned, He took upon Himself the sins of all mankind. The prophet Isaiah prophesied more than 700 years before the earthly ministry of Jesus Christ of the victory that He would win when He died on the cross and subsequently rose from the dead. Isaiah said, "He will swallow up death [in victory; He will abolish death forever]..." (Isaiah 25:8)

Jesus Christ won a total, complete and absolute victory over death. He won this victory for *you*. If you obey God's specific instructions that will be explained in this chapter, you will go to heaven when you die or if you are raptured. Jesus said, "...I am the Way and the Truth and the Life; no one comes to the Father except by (through) Me." (John 14:6)

Please note the important words "no one" in this verse of Scripture. *No* human being can come to God unless that person receives eternal salvation through Jesus Christ.

No human being, no matter how good you may think your life has been, has lived a life that is good enough to live eternally in heaven. "...None is righteous, just and truthful and upright and conscientious, no, not one." (Romans 3:10)

God always emphasizes through repetition. Just a few verses later He emphasizes once again that no human being deserves to live eternally in heaven. Every human being is a sinner. "...all have sinned and are falling short of the honor and glory which God bestows and receives." (Romans 3:23)

If you have not yet received eternal salvation through Jesus Christ and you are reading these words, *you can be absolutely certain that the same God Who created you is drawing you to Him.* Jesus said, " No one is able to come to Me unless the Father Who sent Me attracts and draws him and gives him the desire to come to Me, and [then] I will raise him up [from the dead] at the last day." (John 6:44)

Please note the words "no one" at the beginning of this verse. No person can come to Christ unless God Himself "attracts and draws him and gives him the desire" to come to Christ. God is drawing *you* to Christ at this moment if you have not already received Him as your Savior. If you receive Jesus Christ as your Savior, you will live with Him throughout eternity. Jesus said, "...unless a person is born again (anew, from above), he cannot ever see (know, be acquainted with, and experience) the kingdom of God." (John 3:3)

What do the words "born again" mean? You experienced a physical birth when you were born out of your mother's womb. You must experience a separate spiritual birth to live eternally with Christ.

The Bible explains exactly what you should do to receive eternal salvation through Jesus Christ. "...if you acknowledge and confess with your lips that Jesus is Lord and in your heart believe (adhere to, trust in, and rely on the truth) that God raised Him from the dead, you will be saved. For with the heart a person believes (adheres to, trusts in, and relies on Christ) and so is justified (declared righteous, acceptable to God), and with the mouth he confesses (declares openly and speaks out freely his faith) and confirms [his] salvation." (Romans 10:9-10)

The only way that you can be certain that you will receive eternal salvation through Jesus Christ is to fulfill God's specific instructions in this passage of Scripture. If you *believe in your heart* that God raised Jesus Christ from death *and* if you open your mouth and state this heartfelt belief, you *will* be saved.

You must do more than just think in your *mind* that Jesus Christ was crucified and rose from the dead. God instructs you to believe deep down in your *heart* that He raised Jesus Christ from death for you. If you have absolute faith that Jesus Christ paid the full price for all of your sins, you will be saved. You must confess this heartfelt belief by speaking with your *mouth* what you believe in your heart.

Do you believe in your heart that Jesus Christ is the Son of God, that He gave up His position of equality with God to come to earth as a human being, that He paid the full price for your sins when He died on the cross and that He victoriously rose from death? Will you *open your mouth to express your heartfelt belief by saying*, "I am so grateful. I am absolutely certain that Jesus Christ left His position of equality with God in heaven to come to earth as a human being to die a horrible death by crucifixion to pay the full price for my sins. I know that Jesus Christ victoriously rose from the dead. I know that all of my sins have been paid for and that I will live throughout eternity with Christ. Thank You, Jesus. Thank You, Father."

If you believe this great truth in *your heart* and if you speak this belief with *your mouth*, you are saved. If you spoke these words with your mouth and you believe them in your heart, "Your eyes will see the King in His beauty..." (Isaiah 33:17)

If you have received eternal salvation through Jesus Christ, you will see Him with your own eyes in heaven. If you were not already saved when you began reading this chapter, we pray that you have received eternal salvation through Jesus Christ after reading the scriptural truths in this chapter. *No* decision that you will ever make will even remotely approach the importance of the decision to receive eternal salvation through Jesus Christ.

Conclusion

This book is filled with very important scriptural truths pertaining to the Rapture of the Church, the Tribulation and the Second Coming of Christ. We have written this book to encourage you to live your life from God's perspective, continually drawing closer to Him each day as you understand what He will do in the future.

Please pray about sharing a copy of this book with your friends and loved ones. In order to enable you to purchase several copies of our publications, we provide a 40% discount for 5-9 items and a 50% discount for any 10 or more items. From our beginning God has instructed us to give our readers similar discounts to the discounts that bookstores receive when they purchase books in quantity. See the order form at the back of this book.

If this book has helped you, would you share your testimony with us so that we can share with others what God has done in your life because you read and obeyed the scriptural instructions in *The Rapture and the Second Coming of Christ*? We normally need three to four paragraphs in a testimony so that we can consolidate this information into one solid paragraph for our newsletter and our website. Your comments will encourage many people, including the pastors and leaders in Third World countries and inmates in prisons and jails who receive our books free of charge.

Please send any comments that you have to us at lamplightmin@yahoo.com. You also can mail your comments to Lamplight Ministries, Inc., PO Box 1307, Dunedin, FL 34697.

We invite you to visit our website: www.lamplight.net. You will find many comments from people who have been helped by our books, Scripture cards and CDs. You also will find a section on biblical health as well as recipes that Judy adds each month to bless you. We are in good health at ages 83 and 75. I know that I would not be alive today if it were not for Judy's knowledge and wisdom regarding health and her amazing recipes.

You can keep in touch with us on Facebook (facebook.com/jackandjudylamplight) and Twitter (twitter.com/lamplightmin). You can follow our blog at lamplightmin.wordpress.com You can receive frequent updates on our latest books. You can order our books as e-books at SmashWords.com – enter "Jack Hartman."

We ask you to pray for us. We are completing two books each year with no foreseeable plans to stop delivering God's Word to readers with a simple and easy-to-understand explanation. Your prayers for us will make a difference.

We have been blessed to share with you the results of hundreds of hours that we have invested to learn what the Word of God teaches about the Rapture of the

Church, the Tribulation and the Second Coming of Christ. We will be excited to hear about your journey with Jesus Christ through this book. We are looking forward to hearing from you.

Blessed to be a blessing. (Genesis 12:1-3)

Jack and Judy

Appendix

A Brief Overview of End-Time Events

We are focused in this book on the Rapture and the Second Coming of Jesus Christ. We must put them in context with the other events that will take place. Study for yourself each topic to learn the details of each event. There are different viewpoints on events where the exact time is not given.

- The Rapture (I Thessalonians 4:16-17; Luke 17:34-37; Revelation 3:10; Mark 13:32; I Corinthians 15:52; I Thessalonians 5:9; Daniel 12:1-2; Matthew 24:29-31; Matthew 24:42; Matthew 25:4; Mark 13:32-37; I Thessalonians 5:2; II Thessalonians 2:1; Luke 17:34

- The Judgment Seat of Christ (for believers - II Corinthians 5:10; Romans 14:10-12)

- Marriage of the Lamb and His Bride in heaven (Revelation 19:7-8)

- The Marriage Supper of the Lamb (Revelation 19:9)

- The First 3 ½ years of Tribulation:

  - The Seven Seals (Revelation 6-7)

- Revival during the Tribulation led by 144,000 Jewish evangelists (Revelation 7:1-8)

- The Last 3 ½ years of Tribulation

  - The wrath of God is poured out: Seven trumpets (Revelation 8)

  - Seven bowls: Plagues (Revelation 16)

  - The two witnesses (Revelation 11:1-14)

  - The beast (Antichrist) and the false prophet and those who worshiped him are cast alive into a lake of fire burning with brimstone (Revelation 19:20)

- The Second Coming of Jesus Christ (Matthew 24:27-31; Revelation 19:11-16) a major doctrine of the Bible with 300 references to it in the New Testament; in the Old Testament Daniel, David, Isaiah, Jeremiah and most of the minor prophets refer to the return of Jesus Christ; Jesus Christ Himself taught of His return

- The Battle of Armageddon (Zechariah 12:1-9; Revelation 16:14)

- Satan is bound for 1,000 years, the Millennium (Revelation 20:1)

- The Millennial Reign of Jesus Christ (Revelation 20:1-10; Daniel 2:44; 7:13-14)

- Satan is loosed to deceive the nations (Gog and Magog) and gather an army as numerous as the sand of the sea (Revelation 20:7-8)

- Fire from God in heaven devours them; Satan is cast into the lake of fire (Revelation 20:9-10)

- The Great White Throne Judgment (Revelation 20:11-15) Judgment of unbelievers and then cast into the lake of fire (Luke 16:23-24, 28; Matthew 8:12; Luke 13:28; Matthew 25:46; Hebrews 6:2; Luke 16:27-28)

- The new heavens and the new earth (the New Jerusalem (Revelation 21:1-2; Isaiah 60:1; Isaiah 60:3; Zechariah 16:19)

Study Guide

What Did You Learn From This Book?

The questions in this Study Guide are carefully arranged to show you how much you have learned about the Rapture and the Second Coming of Christ. This Study Guide is not intended to be an academic test. The sole purpose of the following questions is to help you increase your practical knowledge pertaining to the Rapture and the Second Coming of Christ.

Page number

1. Why do unbelievers and some immature Christians look at the scriptural teachings that we are sharing with you in this book as meaningless nonsense? Why are some people incapable of understanding these scriptural truths? (I Corinthians 2:14-15) 11-12

2. There is no doubt that Jesus Christ will come to earth again. What did He say about His Second Coming? (John 14:3) 19

3. How can you be certain that every word in the Bible is inspired by God Who is the Author of

A Few Words About Lamplight Ministries

Lamplight Ministries, Inc. originally began in 1983 as Lamplight Publications. After ten years as a publishing firm with a goal of selling Christian books, Lamplight Ministries was established in 1991. Jack and Judy Hartman founded Lamplight Ministries with a mission of continuing to sell their publications and also to *give* large numbers of these publications free of charge to needy people all over the world.

Lamplight Ministries was created to allow people who have been blessed by our publications to share in financing the translation, printing and distribution of our books into other languages and also to distribute our publications free of charge to inmates in jails and prisons. Over the years many partners of Lamplight Ministries have shared Jack and Judy's vision. Thousands of people in jails and prisons and in Third World countries have received our publications free of charge.

Our books and Scripture Meditation Cards have been translated into eleven foreign languages – Armenian, Danish, Greek, Hebrew, German, Korean, Norwegian, Portuguese, Russian, Spanish and the

Tamil dialect in India. The translations in these languages are not available from Lamplight Ministries in the United States. These translations can only be obtained in the countries where we have given permission for them to be published.

The pastors of many churches in Third World countries have written to say that they consistently preach sermons in their churches based on the scriptural contents of our publications. We believe that people in several churches in *many* different countries hear sermons that are based on the scriptural contents of our publications. Praise the Lord!

Jack Hartman was the sole author of twelve Christian books. After co-authoring one book with Judy, Jack and Judy co-authored ten sets of Scripture Meditation Cards. Judy has been the co-author of every subsequent book. Jack and Judy currently are working on other books that they believe the Lord is leading them to write as co-authors.

We invite you to request our newsletters to stay in touch with us, to learn of our latest publications and to read comments from people all over the world. Please write, fax, call or email us. You are very special to us. We love you and thank God for you. Our heart is to take the gospel to the world and for our books to be available in every known language. Hallelujah!

Lamplight Ministries, Inc.,
PO Box 1307 - Dunedin, Florida, 34697. USA
Phone: 1-800-540-1597
Fax: 1-727-784-2980
website: lamplight.net
email: lamplightmin@yahoo.com

Enthusiastic Comments from Readers of our Publications

The following are just a few of the many comments we have received from people in *61 countries* pertaining to our publications. For additional comments, see our website: lamplight.net.

Trust God for Your Finances

There are more than 150,000 copies of *Trust God for Your Finances* in print. This book has been translated into seven foreign languages.

- "I have translated *Trust God for Your Finances* into Thai. I intended to make about 50 or 60 photocopies of this translation to distribute among friends. My pastor asked for 700 copies to distribute at the special yearly conference for pastors. My immediate thought was that I could not do this, but he urged me to pray and try my best. Surprisingly, it worked out. Thank God. More than 1,000 people attended the conference. Seven hundred copies were distributed to only the pastors, elders and deacons who really wanted the book. After the conference, we had so many calls that another 2,000 copies were printed. Thank you, Mr. Hartman, for this book which is helping so many Thai Christians." (Thailand)

- "I bought your book, *Trust God for Your Finances,* at a church I was attending in Virginia in the 1980s. This book transformed my life. It was all Bible-based and solid in every way. I married a Bulgarian pastor who started the church here during Communism and the underground church. We have pastored together for 22 years. I gave your book to my husband and he consumed it. He kept it near his Bible all the time. God has raised him up to be influential in this nation. He has written a book titled *The Covenant of Provision* dealing with finances. Your book helped him so much to form his ideas about the rightful use of money. This book has influenced my husband more than almost any other book. It was so timely and needed coming out of a Communist society. Thank you so much for this book." (Bulgaria)

- "Today we had a ministry partner join us for lunch. He said that the book, *Trust God for Your Finances,* that we had translated into Hebrew was the most powerful book he had ever read on the subject. I shared with him the wonderful story of how you shared the book with us and how many Israelis have been enlightened in that area as a result of reading the book. You both are a blessing and a treasure in God's kingdom." (Israel)

What Does God Say?
- "Your book *What Does God Say?* is one of the greatest books I have ever read. You tell the truth and back it up with Scripture. I started crime very

young. I have spent a large portion of my life behind bars. I have so much to be ashamed of and things that I am very sorry for. I have almost wasted my life. I say almost because this book caused me to realize that God loves even me no matter what I have done. In your book I read that there is no condemnation in Christ Jesus. Do you have any idea what it means to feel no condemnation when society says to lock me up because I am guilty? My sins and all the crimes I have committed have been washed away. I cannot explain how it feels to know that someone is really proud of me. That someone is Jesus. I am taking this book home with me. Even though I don't have much education, I can understand it very well. I now know that I am saved and I am forgiven. Thank you very much for writing this book." (Florida)

- "Several months ago, you sent me a copy of your book titled *What Does God Say?*. This book is amazing. First of all, I could understand it. My English is not great. I have been a Muslim all my life. I was taught as a child what I was supposed to believe. When I was searching for real truth, I met the Master and received Jesus Christ as my Savior. When I read your book, it filled so much of the void and loneliness that I was filled with. I will be sharing Jesus and *What Does God Say?* with my family and with other Muslims. Please pray for me as I may not be welcomed in my own home town for finding this wonderful Jesus." (Ghana)

- "Our ministry here in South Africa is flourishing. We thank God for the books from Jack and Judy Hartman. The book, *What Does God Say?*, is my daily manual. It addresses all issues of life. I read it every day and I love it. I am complete. This book has made our ministry more effective. I no longer have to struggle on what to preach or teach. I am now equipped with the correct material. This book is filled with the anointing and revelation of God. My fellow pastors here in South Africa are hungry for these books. We soon will be opening a branch in Pretoria and also in Botswana. I thank God for the Hartmans. I always pray for them." (South Africa)

Quiet Confidence in the Lord
- "As soon as I was diagnosed with prostate cancer, I began to meditate on the Scripture and your explanation of the Scripture in *Quiet Confidence in the Lord*. I carried this book with me everywhere for several weeks. The specialist at the Lahey Clinic in Boston told me I was the calmest person with this diagnosis that he had ever seen. During the pre-op and the surgery, a number of people commented on how calm I was. I experienced a lot of discomfort during the difficult first week at home after the surgery. I focused constantly on the Scripture in this wonderful book. I was remarkably calm. Thank you for writing this book that has helped me so much." (Massachusetts)

- "After I graduated from Bible school, I went outside of my country for mission work with my wife. After we were there for nine months, my wife died suddenly. My sorrow was great. I read your book titled *Quiet Confidence in the Lord*. This book spoke to my heart. All twenty-three chapters were written for me. God changed me through this book and comforted me and took away my sorrow. Through the blood of Jesus I entered God's rest. I can give a great recommendation for this book to anyone who is filled with sorrow and grief. I pray that many people will read this book and develop quiet confidence in the Lord as I did. Thank you so much for sending this book to me. May God bless you and your ministry." (Ethiopia)

• *"Quiet Confidence in the Lord* is with me at work each day. I have read and underlined passages that lift my heart and help me to understand something I've known all along and that is that I am not alone and that God cares very much that I'm in the midst of great adversity. I asked God to send me a comforter, someone who would put their arms around me and say, 'I understand and I care.' The answer to that prayer is in you and Judy. Thanks to *Quiet Confidence of the Lord* I am, for the first time in my life, learning to focus on God and not my problems. Thank you both for your ministry. Your books are a tremendous blessing to hurting people all over the world." (Washington, DC)

God's Instructions for Growing Older

• "I am a 63-year-old businesswoman from Thailand. Like most women around the world, I do not like growing old. When I received a copy of your book, *God's Instructions For Growing Older*, I read straight from the first page to the last in two days. Your book gives me the assurance of how to grow older without fear, anxiety, and worry. I will live the rest of my life in peace and joy for I now know that if we keep God in first place at all times, the final years of our lives will be meaningful, productive, and fulfilling. Thank you, Mr. and Mrs. Hartman, for the priceless gift of your book. May God bless you and your team always." (Thailand)

- "I have never read a book like *God's Instructions for Growing Older*. Finally a book has been written that teaches how to finish our course in life as a Christian. Your chapter on Scripture meditation is pure gold. This book is a road map to direct us in the way the Lord intends for us to grow older. Thank you so much for this special book." (Florida)

- "Thank you for your new book, *God's Instructions for Growing Older*. I love this book. I read a little bit every day so that I can be an encourager to my older friends and to myself. We so need God's knowledge during the final years of our lives. I have started my gift list to share this book with others." (Texas)

Receive Healing from the Lord
- "Your great book, *Receive Healing from the Lord*, has amazed me. This book has been my daily bread. I have followed all of God's instructions in your book. My children and my wife were healed from severe illness. I was sick myself just before an important crusade. I meditated on the Scripture in your book for the entire night. I was totally healed. The following day God did wonders as He healed many people. Since then, people have been coming to receive their healing at our home and church almost every day. Many healings are taking place at our

services. This book is wonderful. I am abundantly blessed by it." (Zambia)

- "My husband and I served in the mission field in Swaziland, Africa, for three and a half years. Upon our arrival, Lamplight Ministries sent us four mailbags full of Jack and Judy's books. Because Swaziland is so laden with HIV/AIDS, we were able to use the book, *Receive Healing from the Lord,* with the people in Swaziland to see many people come to a saving knowledge of the Lord Jesus Christ and His perfect will regarding healing. We saw mothers with very sick children who themselves also were afflicted with AIDS respond to the many Scriptures that are part of the book, actually believing that it was meant for them. Had it not been for the use of this book and the other books you sent, we would not have had such success in teaching a Bible study about the truth in God's Word to these people. We gave out your books and told the people that the book was theirs to keep. We saw such joy and surprise on the faces of these impoverished people. We appreciate the ongoing generosity of Lamplight Ministries for 'such a time as this' in these days where there is so much need and want. We will forever be thankful that we can count on the Word of God through the books written by Jack and Judy as effective tools in the transformation of people's lives." (Swaziland)

- "Thank you very much for sending me your book, *Receive Healing from the Lord.* After reading the first chapter I realized that this book could be the solution for my wife's failing health. We decided to read the book together every day. My wife was healed and restored after carefully following the scriptural principles that you explained. We are humbled by how we had struggled and panicked trying to find an answer. God gave us the solution in your book. We are so grateful to you. We love you and we are praying for you." (Zambia)

You Can Hear the Voice of God

- "Many years of my life I scoffed at Christians. I looked at them as holy rollers. When I was incarcerated, I experienced pain as I have never felt in my life. A darkness and loneliness like I have never experienced before came upon me. A friend here gave me your book, *You Can Hear the Voice of God*. If there ever was a time when I needed to hear from God, it is now. My wife was desperately ill at the very point of death when I started reading your book. I now know that God has been trying to talk to me all of my life, but I didn't know how to listen to His voice. NOW I CAN HEAR THE VOICE OF GOD. In a splendid and simple way you actually taught me how to hear the voice of God Almighty. How can I ever thank you? Thank you for writing this book. It will impact hundreds of thousands, I am sure." (Florida)

- "Thank you for sending me a copy of *You Can Hear the Voice of God*. This book is so good. On the first day of having this book in my hands, I read continually. I finished five chapters. My wife was invited to teach at a meeting of pastors' wives. The women were excited because of this teaching. I would like to translate this book into Benba, one of the largest spoken languages on the copper belt and some provinces of Zambia. Would you give me permission to translate this book? I know that the Holy Spirit has inspired me to do so." (Zambia) (Permission was granted.)

- "Thank you for the box of books that you sent to a pastor who is a friend of mine. He gave me a copy of your book *You Can Hear The Voice of God*. This book is a spiritual manual for the serious Christian. I thank God for Jack and Judy Hartman. This book is helping me to draw closer to my Maker. I now realize that God has been talking to me daily but I did not hear Him. This book is a real blessing to the body of Christ." (Ghana)

Glorious Eternal Life in Heaven
- "Greetings in Jesus' mighty name. I am excited to report that *Glorious Eternal Life in Heaven* is one of the best books I have ever read. This book will be a major resource for me as I prepare to teach others that we are free from the bondage of death. God bless you and give you long life to continue to sow the precious seeds of the Word of Life to many people. Be blessed, for great is your reward." (Kenya)

- "Dear Papa Jack and Judy, thank you for sending me a copy of your book, *Glorious Eternal Life in Heaven*. This book is very important and interesting. It is a blessing to me and to our church. I am writing to express my profound gratitude to my heavenly Father for all He has done in my life through this book. This book has helped me and several members of my church who long for a Holy Spirit revival in this town. Anyone facing a life or death struggle will be comforted by this book." (Kenya)

- This pastor said, "Warm greetings in the great name of our Lord and Savior Jesus Christ. Thank you very much for sending me your book, *Glorious Eternal Life in Heaven*. Would you please send me another copy of this book to give to a friend who is a pastor? Your books are my best resources to prepare my preaching and teaching into our local languages. By translating from your books into these languages, I can say that you are serving in many area churches. God bless you all." (Ethiopia)

Effective Prayer

- "I thank God for your book titled *Effective Prayer*. This book came to me at the right time. Since reading this book, God has done great wonders in my life and ministry. Our whole church is being affected by what we have learned about the power of prayer. I have read many books on prayer, but this one is unique. I no longer pray amiss. My prayer life has become much more effective. Your book has helped me to persevere in prayer much longer than before. This is a great book. I love it. I treasure this book. I do not know how to thank you. I pray that God will bless you both with long life and that you will enjoy the fruit of your labour." (Zambia)

- "Your book *Effective Prayer* is a great blessing to me. After reading this book I have so much more understanding about prayer. It is very easy to learn from all that you are teaching and all of the Scriptures in it. I now understand much more about the significance of prayer in my daily life, why I should pray and how to pray. You have enlightened my mind. I know that my loving Father wants me to pray all the time. I have learned to pray God's answer instead of focusing on the problem. This book is very vital to my daily life. I am so thankful to both of you for another great book for people who need answers. Thank you so much for the great understanding that I found in this book." (the Philippines)

- "I have been studying your book *Effective Prayer*. This book has inspired me to do a lot more praying. Praying to God is such a privilege. To know that God is just waiting for me to come and talk with Him is tremendous. The way you brought out the gift of being baptized in the Holy Spirit and praying in tongues will make it easier for people to receive this much-needed gift in their lives. Our pastor is using your book to teach on prayer. I have given copies of this book to many people in our church. I gave one to another pastor in our town. I love you both in the Lord Jesus Christ. I thank God for you and for allowing Him to continue to use you in the body of Christ." (Oklahoma)

Never, Never Give Up
- "I am a 68-year-old businessman. At my age I should be enjoying a life way past retirement. It is not so. In 1997 Thailand suffered a severe economic crunch and my business almost went down under. It took me many years to try to come back. Just as I thought I was climbing out of the black hole, another crisis hit two years ago. This time I am too old to fight, but I have no choice but to go on. I thought that God and I were very close. However, after the first crisis hit I sort of lost my faith along with my hope. After the second crisis hit, I thought that God had forsaken

me. I all but lost my faith totally until one day a good friend gave me a book, *Never, Never Give Up*. At first I didn't want to read it. However, insisted by my friend, I did. I stayed up the whole night finishing the book. By morning I kneeled down and begged God to forgive me for my foolishness. I felt so ashamed for my behavior. I begged Him to accept me back. After I did that, I know that God has forgiven me. Now I am back to feeling close to Him again. I am so happy and grateful for this book. God is great!" (Thailand)

- "Thanks for being there when you are so much needed by all of us. After seven major operations I am beginning to walk again and help others which is the full purpose of my existence which Jesus Christ has set before me. Your book, *Never, Never Give Up*, stayed by my pillow along with my Bible while I was recuperating from these operations. When I re-read it, I was charged with peace and energy again. The pain diminishes and I can speak of God's infinite love and mercy to others who are facing similar trials. Thank you for writing this God-inspired book." (Florida)

- "Suicide has shown its face in my mind. I found myself falling deeper and deeper into the pit of hell. My life seemed so grim. I could not see where I could make a difference and was planning to believe that if I chose to leave this life it would not matter. When I received *Never, Never Give Up* I read the first three chapters that evening. When I arrived at page ninety, your verse changed my life. I want you to know that I have been delivered from this season of trial. I rededicated my life to the Lord and feel wonderful. Thank you so much for your work. Through our Lord you have saved my life. Thank you for my life back." (Texas)

Reverent Awe of God

- "Greetings in the mighty name of our Lord Jesus. Thank you for sending me a free copy of *Reverent Awe of God*. I was surprised to learn your ages when I read this book. You are still relevant in your books. You are changing the destiny of many people globally. I will use this book to teach our church members from the many valuable lessons that I have learned from your book. May God bless you and supply all of your needs." (Kenya)

- "A student in one of the universities read your book, *Reverent Awe of God*, from our library. As a result, she was converted from the Muslim religion to Christianity. She said that the concept of our Christian faith is more real. She can see that God is her Father and that Jesus Christ is real and the only Son of God. This student said that she is facing attacks and rejections from her home. She needs our prayers. Papa, thank you." (Ghana)

- "We are very grateful for the box of books you sent us. I praise God for your new book, *Reverent Awe of God*. This book can really help any believer to establish a genuine relationship with our Maker. When we read your books and consider your age, we thank God that the Spirit of God never grows old. May God continue to bless you and give you long life so that you will write many more books that explain the Word of God to us." (Ghana)

Overcoming Fear

- "Thank you for sending your books to the Philippines. I was very blessed to read *Overcoming Fear*. This book explained the sources of fear and what I should do to overcome fear. It is really a blessing to know all of this information that helped me to overcome the fear I have felt all these years. I have cherished every chapter in the book. It has become food for my soul. Thank you so much for explaining all of this so well. I have learned that I should never be afraid of anyone because I can be absolutely certain that God lives in my heart. This is great assurance because I know that God is greater than anything I will ever face in this life. This book has been a great blessing in my life. God bless you both." (the Philippines)

- "I want to thank you immediately for your new book, *Overcoming Fear*. I have read every one of your books and given copies to many people, but I want to tell you that I believe this is your best book ever. I can hardly put it down. The day I received it I stayed up late, even though I was very tired, to read the first four chapters. The next morning I read two more chapters before going to work. This book is very inspiring. It gives me great peace. God's peace is so great that I cannot describe it. I have almost finished reading this book. When I am done, I will immediately read it again. Enclosed is a check for ten copies of this book plus a contribution to Lamplight Ministries. Thank you, Jack and Judy, for writing this wonderful book." (Massachusetts)

- "I want to thank you for publishing the book *Overcoming Fear*. I am reading mine for the second time. I cannot tell you how comforting it is. The way you have put information along with the right Bible verses is so truly helpful. As world conditions worsen, I can tell you that this book will be a constant companion alongside my Bible. I am so grateful for you both. Keep up the good work. You are making a big difference in peoples' lives. You have in mine." (Minnesota)

Victory Over Adversity
• "I am a pure and proud Dutchman married to a Tanzanian woman. I have had a lot of problems staying with an African wife in Europe. I love my wife so much, but the environment for my wife was not good enough in terms of getting a job. This affected us very much to the extent that I was even planning to relocate to Tanzania for the sake of my wife and children's future. Thank God that an angel was sent to me by the name of Jim who gave me a book, *Victory over Adversity*. This book is amazing and great. It contains the answers to my problems and is a great encouragement to me. As a Dutchman I find it very interesting to read a book with simple English. Putting the facts of this book into practice has changed my life greatly. I have found a new job. My wife has found a good job. The thoughts of relocating to Tanzania have faded. My faith has increased and my commitment to God has grown. I pray that God will bless the writers of this book and also the man who gave me this book. My wife and I are always reading this book. It is our source of strength." (Holland)

- "I praise God for His living Word. Thank you for the books that you have sent to China. You cannot imagine what *Victory over Adversity* did in my life as a young believer. Not only is the language clear and accessible, but the content is very rewarding. I learned a lot from this book. I now meditate day and night on the Word of God. I am in the presence of God often. I am confident that I can overcome any adversity in the precious name of Jesus Christ. May God bless you and fill you with His infinite grace, Mr. Jack and his wife." (China)

- "I am a 22-year-old college student in Thailand. My family is half Christian. My mother is a Christian whereas my father is a Buddhist. I am the eldest daughter of my parents with one younger brother and sister. All three of us have been baptized as Christians since birth. Frankly, I have never had much faith in God and always have had problems with both of my parents. I think that they don't understand me. They think I don't listen to them. Last month my mother was given a book, *Victory over Adversity,* by her friend. Out of curiosity I took the book and read it before she did. I could not put it down. For the first time I felt that God is real and is close to me. I cried and cried and felt sorry for my past behavior toward God and my parents. I went to my mother and apologized, to her great surprise. Now I go to church with her every Sunday. I am very thankful to my mother's friend who gave her this book and also to the writers of this book who have changed my life and brought me to God which my mother could not do. Thank you both!" (Thailand)

- *"Exchange Your Worries for God's Perfect Peace* is a masterpiece. I am reading this book to the people here in the Philippines. I saw tears flowing down their faces as I read them parts of this book. I must get this book translated into their language. I am reading this book for the second time. After 30 years in the ministry I have finally learned how to turn my worries over to God. I have learned more from this book in the last few months than I have ever learned in my life. I will not allow my copy of this book to leave my presence. I thank God for you." (the Philippines)

- "I just want to tell you how much I appreciate you and your excellent book, *Exchange Your Worries for God's Perfect Peace*. I have read all of your books several times each. I continually go back to refer to the notes I have made in your books. I have done this for close to 15 years and pages are falling out of your books. I read the Bible daily. Your books are a close second to the Bible. I have never found another Christian author who teaches me more about God's Word and speaks directly to my heart as your writings do. Thank you for helping me appreciate and respect the Word of God." (Wisconsin)

- "I was in despair struggling with my life and ministry. *Exchange Your Worries for God's Perfect Peace* has strengthened me and encouraged my heart. My country is often threatened by disasters. Your book and the Scripture in it has helped me to focus on God, no matter what circumstances I have experienced and will face in the future. The language in the book is very clear and easy to understand for someone like me who uses English as a second language. I have been blessed by reading this book. My faith in Jesus has increased. Thank you for sending this book to me. I thank God that I know you. You are a blessing." (Indonesia)

God's Joy Regardless of Circumstances

• "*God's Joy Regardless of Circumstances* came to me right on time. Being in prison for 20 years for a crime I didn't commit and then having to deal with severe family problems is not a morsel that is easy to swallow. My oldest daughter was pregnant and we were looking forward to having my first grandson born. We were very pained to learn that my daughter had to lose her baby. In the midst of dealing with this problem, you sent me a free copy of *God's Joy Regardless of Circumstances*. When I avidly started to read this book, my daughter underwent surgery, lost her baby and faced uncertainty and despair. *God's Joy Regardless of Circumstances* pulled us through. Thank you also for sending a free copy of this book to my daughter. May God continue blessing Lamplight Ministries." (Florida)

• "Many thanks for sending me *God's Joy Regardless of Circumstances*. This book has been a real stream in the desert that I have been able to drink from. I have been blessed tremendously by this book. My life has not been the same since I started reading it. I have used this book to help many people on my radio programme every Sunday. Many people have given their lives to Christ because of these messages." (Zambia)

- "Only this year I faced a lot of challenges. As a result I became bitter at heart. The wonderful Scripture verses in *God's Joy Regardless of Circumstances* took away my bitterness. I am happy now. This book has instructed me how to handle any situation with God's joy. I now can see God's solution to my life challenges by the presence of God's joy inside me. Your God-given insight has given new meaning to my spiritual life. Thank you for the encouragement through your writings." (Lome-Togo West Africa)

God's Wisdom Is Available to You
- "I did not sleep last night after reading your book *God's Wisdom is Available to You.* Thank you for your wonderful work. Because of persecution against my ministry, I spent a considerable amount of time in the hospital because of depression. I am now well and healthy in Jesus' name. Thank you for your help. I will be teaching members of my church from key text in your book. Please be my mentor, teacher and counselor." (Ghana)

- "I thank God each and every day for Jack and Judy Hartman. When I started reading your book on wisdom, everything was going wrong in my life. This book revived my spirit and my faith in God. It has changed my life. The Bible used to be like Greek to me. Now I can read it and understand it. I can't put this book down because I know I need to absorb it. I'm going through it for a second time. This book is one of the best things that has ever happened to me. I thank you both and I thank God." (Florida)

- "You did a fantastic job on this book. It is an encyclopedia on God's wisdom. The writing style is just great. Many books don't bring the reader through the subject the way this book does. I'm very impressed with that. You have made it a real joy for me to study and re-digest Scripture. This book has been very good for me." (North Carolina)

A Close and Intimate Relationship with God

- "Your book, *A Close and Intimate Relationship with God,* is tremendous. I thought that I had a close relationship with God, but this book really opened my eyes. I now can see many things that I still need to do to be even closer to God. I couldn't put this book down. When I had to stop reading, I couldn't wait to get back to it the next day. Every chapter is filled with Scripture that is very helpful to me. I will be making many changes in my life as a result of reading this awesome book. Thank you and God bless you." (New Hampshire)

- "Thank you for giving me a copy of your book *A Close and Intimate Relationship with God.* This book is written so clearly that all instructions are to the point. My life has been greatly changed and refreshed. The presence of God has become very strong in my life. I am at peace trusting my God to meet every need. My mind is totally on God. I can clearly hear His voice. I am receiving guidance and direction from Him as a result of this book. I cannot afford to spend a day without reading this book. I carry it with me wherever I go." (Zambia)

- "Thank you for your book titled *A Close and Intimate Relationship with God.* This inspiring book helped me to draw closer to our heavenly Father. In Chapter 25 you said that Paul and Silas were praising God in prison. I was having a challenging day when I read this chapter. God spoke through your book to praise Him no matter what circumstances I faced. Thank you for that inspiration. The information on dying to self in the last chapter where Paul said that he dies daily really encouraged me. I am learning to do much better putting God first, others second and myself last. Thank you at Lamplight Ministries for the thousands of people around the world that you are supporting. May the dear Lord bless you abundantly." (China)

Unshakable Faith in Almighty God
- "I thank God for the book *Unshakable Faith in Almighty God*. Because I am not indigenous Chinese, it is not easy to fellowship with the local Chinese. When I got this book I was able to see a way in the wilderness. It became my guide and light every day. When I was just about to give up Christianity, God at the right time provided this book to me. The truths and clear instruction in this book are direct from the throne of God. I am determined to move on with God come what may. I praise God that is He able to raise people we have never seen like Jack and Judy Hartman to speak into our lives through their publications. God bless the Hartman family. One day when Christ comes it will be exciting for them to see how they have influenced the world for God in Jesus' name. I am so grateful for these free books that cost a lot of money in publishing, printing and postage." (China)
- "I have been pastoring in Belgium for the past 15 years. In the past our church was flourishing and

doing very well until late last year when my praise and worship leader decided to break away and form another church. This was a very big blow to us as a church. Most of our strong and committed members left the church with some of the church instruments. My wife almost gave up. She was discouraged. This also affected our finances. Pastor Jim gave me a book titled *Unshakable Faith in Almighty God*. Before I read this book my faith was shaken and I almost gave up. This book took me step by step to show me how to make my faith grow. You cannot read this book and remain the same. I have been using the book to preach to the few members that remain with us. In the past four months we have experienced revival. The anointing is so strong and the members have been strengthened so much through the preaching from this book. We are determined to not give up. God bless the Hartmans for being a blessing to us in Europe." (Belgium)

- "*Unshakable Faith in Almighty God* has amazed me. The language is so simple and very clear to understand. This book is powerful and life-changing. I will always hang on to this book. Brother Hartman, God's favour and wisdom are so great on your life. I believe this book is written on very heavy anointing from God. Your reward in heaven will be so great. All those who have sown seeds in your ministry should rejoice. When I wake up, I read this book. Before going to bed, I read it. I will continue to go through it again and again. Your ministry is a big blessing to me. You are always in our prayers." (Zambia)

How to Study the Bible

- "Your book, *How to Study the Bible,* is a gem. Since I became a Christian 41 years ago, I have studied the Bible using a variety of methods. Your method is simple and straightforward. It involves hard work, but the rewards are real. I have read several of your books and this book is the one I would highly recommend to any Christian because this book is the foundation. God bless you, brother." (England)

- "My wife and I are utilizing the Bible study method that you explained in *How to Study the Bible.* We are really growing spiritually as a result. Our old methods of study were not nearly as fruitful. Thank you for writing about your method." (Idaho)

- "I have read almost all of your books and they are outstanding. The one that blessed me the most was *How to Study the Bible.* The study part was excellent, but the meditation chapters were very, very beneficial. I am indebted to you for sharing these. I purchased 30 copies to give to friends. Every earnest student of God's Word needs a copy." (Tennessee)

Increased Energy and Vitality

- "It is so great to meet Christians on the same wave length. In your book *Increased Energy and Vitality,* you are writing almost word for word in some cases what I have been saying to patients for almost 30 years." (Ohio)

- "Last year I obtained a copy of your book *Increased Energy and Vitality.* My wife and I have read and have in fact changed our ways of eating and drinking and exercising because of your influence. We thoroughly appreciate this God-centered message that is so well presented. I have enclosed an order for more of these books. We know many people we wish to help. This is the first step in spreading the news you have so generously put together. Thank you for your efforts. May God continue your leadership in writing, speaking and guidance." (Illinois)

- "I have benefited tremendously from reading and personally applying the principles learned from your book *Increased Energy and Vitality.* By applying your methods, I have gained additional energy especially during my low periods from 2:00 p.m. to 4:00 p.m. I highly recommend your book to others. Keep up the good work." (Florida)

100 Years from Today
- "*100 Years From Today* told me that going to church and doing good deeds won't get me to heaven. I believe in Jesus Christ. I believe He died for our sins and that He forgives us for what we did wrong. Heaven is where I belong. I am born again. I have a new life. This book has changed my life." (Florida)
- "I am writing to express my deep and profound appreciation for your book *100 Years from Today.* I recently began attending a Bible-based church where I found a copy of this book in their lending library. I read the book in one sitting, reading the words aloud to myself. Your book explained details from the Bible that I had not learned before. I thank you for taking the time and effort to write this book. My written words can never fully express how grateful I am to you. By my actions, a changed life

and a deep sense of peace, I hope to bear fruit by helping others." (Massachusetts)

- "I find it hard to put *100 Years from Today* down. I read the whole book in a day and a half. I never knew how much pain and suffering Jesus went through to pay for my sins. I learned how much He loves us." (Florida)

Nuggets of Faith

- "Your books, tapes and meditation cards are really a blessing to me. They came at just the right time. I am preparing sermons on faith from *Nuggets of Faith*. I want the congregation to be constantly learning God's Word in order to have much more faith. I also have been encouraged personally through that book. It is awesome. Thank you for your powerful and inspiring publications." (Zambia)

- "We give *Nuggets of Faith* to people who are hospitalized, for birthdays, to saved and unsaved. Everyone who has received one tells us 'It's the best little book I've ever read. It's so clear and easy to understand.'" (Indiana)

- "I work as a store manager. Today I was told that I was no longer needed. Praise Jesus that only two months prior to this date I had accepted the Lord Jesus as my personal Lord and Savior. I have faith that the Lord was working to bring me to a new direction. I am writing to thank you for your excellent book *Nuggets of Faith*. The moment I arrived home after having been dismissed, I received this book in the mail. I completed this short but awesome book in a little over two hours. It has helped my faith to grow stronger and I know that I will begin a great new journey tomorrow. God bless you." (New York)

Comments on our Scripture Meditation Cards

- "My back was hurting so badly that I couldn't get comfortable. I was miserable whether I sat or stood or laid down. I didn't know what to do. Suddenly I thought of the Scripture cards on healing that my husband had purchased. I decided to meditate on the Scripture in these cards. I was only on the second card when, all of a sudden, I felt heat go from my neck down through my body. The Lord had healed me. I never knew it could happen so fast. The pain has not come back." (Idaho)

- "My wife and I use your Scripture cards every day when we pray. I read the card for that day in English and then my wife repeats it in Norwegian. We then pray based upon the Scripture reference on that day's card. These cards have been very beneficial to us. We would like to see the Scripture cards published in the Norwegian language." (Norway)

- "Your Scripture cards have been very helpful to my wife and myself. We have taped them to the walls in our home and we meditate on them constantly. I also take four or five cards with me every day when I go to work. I meditate on them while I drive. The Scripture on these cards is a constant source of encouragement to us. We ask for permission to translate *Trust God for Your Finances*. This book is badly needed by the people in Turkey." (This permission was granted.) (Turkey)

- "My mom is 95 years old. She was in the Bergen-Belsen Concentration Camp in Germany from 1943 to 1945. She has always had a lot of worry and fear. My mother was helped greatly in overcoming this problem by your Scripture cards titled *Freedom from Worry and Fear*. She was helped so much that she asked me to order another set to give to a friend." (California)

- "I am overwhelmed about the revelations in your Scripture Meditation Cards. These Scripture cards have helped me so much that I cannot write enough on this sheet of paper. We have gone through a five-day programme in our church using the Scripture cards. My faith has increased tremendously. I no longer am submitting to my own will and desires, but I am now submitting to the will of God and it is so fantastic. God bless you, Jack and Judy Hartman." (Ghana)

- "I am very enthusiastic about your Scripture cards and your tape titled *Receive Healing from the Lord*. I love your tape. The clarity of your voice and your sincerity and compassion will encourage sick people. They can listen to this tape throughout the day, before they go to sleep at night, while they are driving to the doctor's office, in the hospital, etc. The tape is filled with Scripture and many good comments on Scripture. This cassette tape and your Scripture cards on healing are powerful tools that will help many sick people." (Tennessee) (NOTE: The ten cassette tapes for our Scripture Meditation Cards are available on 60-minute CDs as well.)

- "I meditate constantly on the healing cards and listen to your tape on healing over and over. Your voice is so soothing. You are a wonderful teacher. My faith is increasing constantly." (New Hampshire).

- "I thank God for you. I carry your Scripture Meditation Cards in my purse. The Scriptures you have chosen are all powerful. What a blessing to be able to meditate on the Word of God at any time, anywhere. Thank you for your hard work. The Scripture cards are a blessing to me." (Canada)

ORDER FORM FOR BOOKS

Book Title	Quantity	Total
What Does God Say? ($18)	_____ x $18 =	_____
The Rapture and the Second Coming of Christ ($14)	_____ x $14 =	_____
Live Continually in the Presence of God ($14)	_____ x $14 =	_____
Glorious Eternal Life in Heaven ($14)	_____ x $14 =	_____
Reverent Awe of God ($14)	_____ x $14 =	_____
God's Plan for Your Life ($14)	_____ x $14 =	_____
You Can Hear the Voice of God ($14)	_____ x $14 =	_____
God's Instructions for Growing Older ($14)	_____ x $14 =	_____
Effective Prayer ($14)	_____ x $14 =	_____
Overcoming Fear ($14)	_____ x $14 =	_____
A Close and Intimate Relationship with God ($14)	_____ x $14 =	_____
God's Joy Regardless of Circumstances ($14)	_____ x $14 =	_____
Victory Over Adversity ($14)	_____ x $14 =	_____
Receive Healing from the Lord ($14)	_____ x $14 =	_____
Unshakable Faith in Almighty God ($14)	_____ x $14 =	_____
Exchange Your Worries for God's Perfect Peace ($14)	_____ x $14 =	_____
God's Wisdom is Available to You ($14)	_____ x $14 =	_____
Quiet Confidence in the Lord ($14)	_____ x $14 =	_____
Never, Never Give Up ($14)	_____ x $14 =	_____
Increased Energy and Vitality ($14)	_____ x $14 =	_____
Trust God For Your Finances ($14)	_____ x $14 =	_____
How to Study the Bible ($10)	_____ x $10 =	_____
Nuggets of Faith ($10)	_____ x $10 =	_____
100 Years From Today ($10)	_____ x $10 =	_____

Price of books _____

Minus 40% discount for 5-9 books _____

Minus 50% discount for 10 or more books _____

Net price of order _____

Add 15% **before discount** for shipping and handling _____

Florida residents only, add 7% sales tax _____

Tax deductible contribution to Lamplight Ministries, Inc. _____

Enclosed check or money order (do not send cash) _____

(Foreign orders must be submitted in U.S. dollars.)

Please make check payable to **Lamplight Ministries, Inc**. and mail to:
PO Box 1307, Dunedin, FL 34697

MC_____ Visa_____ AmEx_____ Disc._____ Card # _____

Exp Date _____ 3-digit code _____ Signature _____

Name _____

Address _____

City _____ Phone _____

State or Province _____ Zip or Postal Code _____

Email _____ Website: _____

ORDER FORM FOR BOOKS

Book Title	Quantity	Total
What Does God Say? ($18)	_____ x $18 =	_____
The Rapture and the Second Coming of Christ ($14)	_____ x $14 =	_____
Live Continually in the Presence of God ($14)	_____ x $14 =	_____
Glorious Eternal Life in Heaven ($14)	_____ x $14 =	_____
Reverent Awe of God ($14)	_____ x $14 =	_____
God's Plan for Your Life ($14)	_____ x $14 =	_____
You Can Hear the Voice of God ($14)	_____ x $14 =	_____
God's Instructions for Growing Older ($14)	_____ x $14 =	_____
Effective Prayer ($14)	_____ x $14 =	_____
Overcoming Fear ($14)	_____ x $14 =	_____
A Close and Intimate Relationship with God ($14)	_____ x $14 =	_____
God's Joy Regardless of Circumstances ($14)	_____ x $14 =	_____
Victory Over Adversity ($14)	_____ x $14 =	_____
Receive Healing from the Lord ($14)	_____ x $14 =	_____
Unshakable Faith in Almighty God ($14)	_____ x $14 =	_____
Exchange Your Worries for God's Perfect Peace ($14)	_____ x $14 =	_____
God's Wisdom is Available to You ($14)	_____ x $14 =	_____
Quiet Confidence in the Lord ($14)	_____ x $14 =	_____
Never, Never Give Up ($14)	_____ x $14 =	_____
Increased Energy and Vitality ($14)	_____ x $14 =	_____
Trust God For Your Finances ($14)	_____ x $14 =	_____
How to Study the Bible ($10)	_____ x $10 =	_____
Nuggets of Faith ($10)	_____ x $10 =	_____
100 Years From Today ($10)	_____ x $10 =	_____

Price of books _____

Minus 40% discount for 5-9 books _____

Minus 50% discount for 10 or more books _____

Net price of order _____

Add 15% **before discount** for shipping and handling _____

Florida residents only, add 7% sales tax _____

Tax deductible contribution to Lamplight Ministries, Inc. _____

Enclosed check or money order (do not send cash) _____

(Foreign orders must be submitted in U.S. dollars.)

Please make check payable to **Lamplight Ministries, Inc**. and mail to:
PO Box 1307, Dunedin, FL 34697

MC_____ Visa_____ AmEx_____ Disc._____ Card # _____

Exp Date _____ 3-digit code _____ Signature _____

Name _____

Address _____

City _____ Phone _____

State or Province _____ Zip or Postal Code _____

Email _____ Website: _____

ORDER FORM FOR SCRIPTURE MEDITATION CARDS AND CDs

SCRIPTURE MEDITATION CARDS	QUANTITY	PRICE
A Closer Relationship with the Lord ($5)	_____	_____
Continually Increasing Faith in God ($5)	_____	_____
Enjoy God's Wonderful Peace ($5)	_____	_____
Financial Instructions from God ($5)	_____	_____
Find God's Will for Your Life ($5)	_____	_____
Freedom from Worry and Fear ($5)	_____	_____
God is Always with You ($5)	_____	_____
Our Father's Wonderful Love ($5)	_____	_____
Receive God's Blessing in Adversity ($5)	_____	_____
Receive Healing from the Lord ($5)	_____	_____

CDs	QUANTITY	PRICE
A Closer Relationship with the Lord ($10)	_____	_____
Continually Increasing Faith in God ($10)	_____	_____
Enjoy God's Wonderful Peace ($10)	_____	_____
Financial Instructions from God ($10)	_____	_____
Find God's Will for Your Life ($10)	_____	_____
Freedom from Worry and Fear ($10)	_____	_____
God is Always with You ($10)	_____	_____
Our Father's Wonderful Love ($10)	_____	_____
Receive God's Blessing in Adversity ($10)	_____	_____
Receive Healing from the Lord ($10)	_____	_____

TOTAL PRICE _____

Minus 40% discount for 5-9 Scripture Cards and CDs
Minus 50% discount for 10 or more Scripture Cards and CDs _____
Net price of order _____
Add 15% **before discount** for shipping and handling _____
Florida residents only, add 7% sales tax _____
Tax deductible contribution to Lamplight Ministries, Inc. _____
Enclosed check or money order (do not send cash) _____
(Foreign orders must be submitted in U.S. dollars.)

Please make check payable to **Lamplight Ministries, Inc**. and mail to:
PO Box 1307, Dunedin, FL 34697

MC_____ Visa_____ AmEx_____ Disc._____ Card # _____

Exp Date _____ 3-digit code _____ Signature _____

Name _____

Address _____

City _____ Phone _____

State or Province _____ Zip or Postal Code _____

Email _____ Website: _____

ORDER FORM FOR SCRIPTURE MEDITATION CARDS AND CDs

SCRIPTURE MEDITATION CARDS	QUANTITY	PRICE
A Closer Relationship with the Lord ($5)	_____	_____
Continually Increasing Faith in God ($5)	_____	_____
Enjoy God's Wonderful Peace ($5)	_____	_____
Financial Instructions from God ($5)	_____	_____
Find God's Will for Your Life ($5)	_____	_____
Freedom from Worry and Fear ($5)	_____	_____
God is Always with You ($5)	_____	_____
Our Father's Wonderful Love ($5)	_____	_____
Receive God's Blessing in Adversity ($5)	_____	_____
Receive Healing from the Lord ($5)	_____	_____

CDs	QUANTITY	PRICE
A Closer Relationship with the Lord ($10)	_____	_____
Continually Increasing Faith in God ($10)	_____	_____
Enjoy God's Wonderful Peace ($10)	_____	_____
Financial Instructions from God ($10)	_____	_____
Find God's Will for Your Life ($10)	_____	_____
Freedom from Worry and Fear ($10)	_____	_____
God is Always with You ($10)	_____	_____
Our Father's Wonderful Love ($10)	_____	_____
Receive God's Blessing in Adversity ($10)	_____	_____
Receive Healing from the Lord ($10)	_____	_____

TOTAL PRICE _____

Minus 40% discount for 5-9 Scripture Cards and CDs

Minus 50% discount for 10 or more Scripture Cards and CDs _____

Net price of order _____

Add 15% **before discount** for shipping and handling _____

Florida residents only, add 7% sales tax _____

Tax deductible contribution to Lamplight Ministries, Inc. _____

Enclosed check or money order (do not send cash) _____

(Foreign orders must be submitted in U.S. dollars.)

Please make check payable to **Lamplight Ministries, Inc**. and mail to:
PO Box 1307, Dunedin, FL 34697

MC_____ Visa_____ AmEx_____ Disc._____ Card # _____

Exp Date _____ 3-digit code _____ Signature _____

Name _____

Address _____

City _____ Phone _____

State or Province _____ Zip or Postal Code _____

Email _____ Website: _____

www.ingramcontent.com/pod-product-compliance
Lightning Source LLC
LaVergne TN
LVHW051132080426
835510LV00018B/2377